What Did You Expect?

Lessons on Spiritual Honesty

by Umm Zakiyyah

Table of Contents

Glossary of Common Arabic and Islamic Terms

adab: good manners; showing others humble respect; Islamic etiquette

alhamdulillah: "All praise belongs to Allah (God, the Creator) alone"

Allah: Arabic term for God; the only One who has the right to be worshipped

'aqeedah: foundational beliefs of the Islamic spiritual way of life

ayaat: plural form of *ayah*

ayah: verse from Qur'an or divine sign

'ayn: (literally "eye") used in reference to "the evil eye," which is often rooted in harmful envy or unhealthy admiration of someone devoid of mentioning Allah

bid'ah: sinful innovation in religion

bi'idhnillaah: "with the help of Allah (the Creator)"

da'wah: teaching others about Islam; inviting others to spiritual guidance

deen: spiritual way of life; religion

dhikr: sincere mention or remembrance of Allah (the Creator)

dhulm: wrongdoing or oppression (of others or one's own soul)

du'aa: prayerful supplication; informal prayer

dunya: this worldly life as opposed to the Hereafter

emaan: sincere faith; authentic spirituality; belief in Islam; *Tawheed*

faahishah: immorality, usually of a sexual nature

faasiq: evildoer; a person living in open sin or wrongdoing

fatwa: Islamic ruling or opinion given by a scholar

fisq: evil, corruption, or clear sin and wrongdoing

fitnah: difficult trial

fitrah: inherent inborn nature of every human soul to worship Allah alone and to live a spiritually and morally upright life

ghayb: unseen

gheebah: backbiting; saying anything about a fellow Muslim that if they were to hear it, they would dislike it

ghuroor: spiritual self-deception

halaal: divinely blessed or permissible

haraam: divinely forbidden or sinful

hasad: envy that is sinful and spiritually destructive *hasan:* good; often used in reference to the rating of "good" regarding the strength of authenticity of a prophetic hadith

hijrah: migration from one land to another for the sake of your faith; moving from a place that harms the soul to a place that nourishes the soul

hikmah: divine wisdom or divinely-inspired wisdom

iftaar: the moment of breaking one's fast at sunset

ijmaa': unanimous agreement amongst the earliest Muslims and scholars

ijtihaad: the process of a qualified scholar (or "*mujtahid*") coming to a religious conclusion on an issue that does not have a clearly defined ruling in the Qur'an or prophetic teachings

istighfaar: uttering supplications seeking Allah's forgiveness

Istikhaarah: prayer and supplication for making a decision about something

istislaam: spiritual surrender

jahiliyyah: pre-Islamic days of spiritual and moral ignorance before the prophetic assignment was given to Prophet Muhammad (peace be upon him); any mindset or life path that mirrors this spiritual and moral ignorance

Jahannam: Hellfire (also called Hell)

Jannah: Paradise (also called Heaven)

kaafir: disbeliever; any person who rejects a foundational part of Islam or *emaan*

khaashi'oon: people who are defined by their *khushoo'*; those who are sincerely and humbly submissive in their worship and obedience to Allah

khushoo': sincerity and humility of the heart and soul; deep concentration in *Salaah* such that the heart is consistently spiritually nourished by its sincere and humble connection to its Creator in every part of prayer

kibr: sinful pride or pride that is spiritually harmful; looking down on others and rejecting the truth

kufr: disbelief; spiritual blasphemy; any belief, speech or action that cancels one's *emaan*

Laa ilaaha illaa Allah: statement of *Tawheed* or declaration of faith that means, "Nothing has the right to be worshipped except Allah alone"

madhloom: one who has been wronged, oppressed, or suffered from *dhulm nafs*: inner-self or desires that are self-serving and spiritually harmful

nameemah: gossip or tale-carrying

naseehah: sincere advice offered to inspire soul-nourishment and life betterment in the one being advised

qadar: divine decree; predestination

qawwaam: the man's divinely assigned role of being the maintainer, provider, and protector of women in the home and society

Qiyaam ul-Layl: the blessed night prayer, prayed in last third of night

Rabb: another name for Allah that refers to His Lordship over creation; Creator, Owner and Manager of all that exists

rak'ah: one unit of *Salaah* (formal prayer)

riba: usury

riyaa: insincerity; showing off; seeking the pleasure, admiration, reward, or attention of other than Allah

ruqyaa: spiritual healing that includes reciting the Qur'an over someone and/or reciting *dhikr* and prayerful supplications for the purpose of healing illness or removing the effects of *'ayn* or *sihr* on someone

sabr: sincere patience; patiently persevering upon that which benefits one's life and soul, and patiently persevering in abstaining from that which harms one's life and the soul

sadaqah: voluntary, non-obligatory charity

sahih/saheeh: authentic; the highest grade of a hadith's authenticity

sajdah: prostrating the forehead on the floor in submission to Allah

Salaah: the five foundational prayers: *Fajr, Dhuhr, 'Asr, Maghrib,* and *'Ishaa'*; second pillar of Islam; formal prayer, whether optional or obligatory

sallallaahu'alayhi wa sallam: prayers of peace and blessing (upon the Prophet)

shahaadah: formal declaration of faith that marks one's entry into Islam: "I bear witness that nothing has the right to be worshipped except Allah alone, and I bear witness that Muhammad is His slave and messenger"; sincere testimony of *Tawheed* recited repeatedly throughout a Muslim's life

Shaytaan: the devil; Satan

shirk: assigning divine attributes to creation or creation's attributes to the Creator

shukr: sincere gratefulness, thankfulness or gratitude

sihr: often referred to as "black magic": when someone works with the jinn to harm someone or get a specific outcome in this world

SubhaanAllah: statement of glorification of Allah: "Glory to Allah, and Exalted and High is He above any imperfection"

sujood: another term for *sajdah*: prostrating the forehead on the floor in submission to Allah

Sunnah: prophetic guidance, teachings, or life example

Sunni: a description of Muslims who affiliate with understanding and living Islam based on the prophetic Sunnah

tafseer: authentic interpretation and spiritual explanation of the *ayaat* of Qur'an

tajweed: rules of reciting the Qur'an based on one or more of the seven authentic prophetic recitation styles

taqwaa: sincere God-consciousness and daily soul care that protects the heart from corruption and the soul from spiritual harm in the Hereafter; fear of Allah

tawakkul: sincere trust in the wisdom and decisions of the Creator

tawbah: sincere repentance; turning one's life around as a form of seeking forgiveness for past sins and wrongdoing

Tawheed: Oneness of Allah; singling out the Creator alone in worship; authentic monotheism; sincere belief in the Oneness of Allah

tazkiyyatun-nafs: purification of the soul; spiritual nourishment that is attained through sincerity while fulfilling the required and optional acts of worship in Islam

'ulamaa: scholars; people of spiritual knowledge (plural of *'aalim*)

ummah: worldwide faith community

uswah: example or pattern to be followed by others

Witr: highly recommended prayer performed after *Ishaa'* or at the closing of *Qiyaam ul-Layl* and consists of three units of prayer (odd number)

wudhoo': ritual ablution that is done before *Salaah*

zakaah/zakaat: obligatory charity paid from one's wealth and given to the needy

zina: fornication or adultery

Author's Note

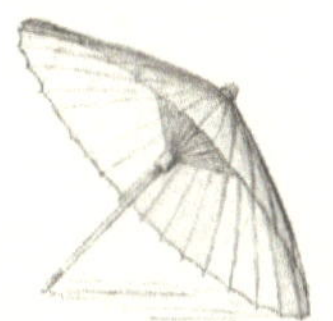

I titled this book *What Did You Expect?* because so many of our emotional and spiritual trials are due to life not going as we expected. As a result, our hearts suffer not only the natural pain that is threaded throughout any worldly trial, but also the additional pain of our own mental distress, emotional frustration, and spiritual confusion.

In this book of reflective prose, I share a collection of spiritual lessons that I learned throughout my own trials of life. Each lesson is shared under the broad umbrella of seven themes that are at the root of my lessons of life and soul. These are lessons that continue to inspire me to strive for spiritual honesty of the heart.

I pray you find in this collection a benefit and inspiration on your own life path.

Your sister in faith and struggle,

August 4th, 2020
14th of Dhul-Hijjah 1441 AH

يَٰٓأَيُّهَا ٱلنَّاسُ إِنَّ وَعْدَ ٱللَّهِ حَقٌّ فَلَا تَغُرَّنَّكُمُ ٱلْحَيَوٰةُ ٱلدُّنْيَا وَلَا يَغُرَّنَّكُم بِٱللَّهِ ٱلْغَرُورُ ٥

"O mankind! Verily, the Promise of Allah is true. So let not this present life deceive you, and let not the chief deceiver [Satan] deceive you about Allah."
—Qur'an (*Faatir*, 35:5)

For those patiently awaiting release from this worldly prison.

"I heard that taqwaa—God-consciousness, fear of Allah, and daily soul-care—is like an umbrella. It shields your soul from spiritual harm like an umbrella shields your body from the rain. And given my continuous spiritual struggles in life, I find this analogy quite apt. Not because I always have that shield, but because I don't. Like most people, I keep an umbrella in my possession, but not always in reach. I usually remember it only on rainy days, because that's the only time I truly appreciate how much I need it. And no matter how often I put it where I think I can find it, I continuously find myself frantically searching for it when I need it most. Unfortunately, there are times in my life that taqwaa has been like that for me. And I no longer want to be in the midst of a storm before I realize how much I need what I should have kept close all along."
—from the journal of Umm Zakiyyah

Lesson One

Is Your Idea of Happiness and Success Spiritually Honest?

"You have to care about your soul more than you care about the specifics of the temporary comforts and tests God will give you in this world. That's what it boils down to. This is what we need to teach our hearts, and this is what we need to teach our souls…"
—from the journal of Umm Zakiyyah

1

Comforts and Tests

"I can't do this anymore," the woman told me. "All this praying and fasting and staying away from sex, hoping I'll get married one day. What's the point? I'm thirty years old, and I don't even know how it feels to be touched. And right now, all I want is for a man to touch me. What if I never get married?" she said.

"All those things we're taught about being patient and obeying Allah so we can have a good life aren't true," she vented. "I haven't experienced any of it. But you know who has? All my friends who broke every rule. While I was praying, they were partying. While I was fasting, they were feasting. While I was lowering my gaze and being a 'good Muslim girl,' they were out sleeping around," she said, frustration evident in her tone.

"But now they're the ones with husbands and children and big houses and lots of money," she complained. "Meanwhile I'm alone, broke, and with no marriage prospect in sight. So I don't see the point in following the rules anymore. All it's brought me is misery and loneliness."

It broke my heart listening to my Muslim sister's emotional pain. I wished I could take the pain away. I wished I could tell her that she'd have everything she dreamed of one day. But I couldn't. So I just told her the truth, the truth she should have been taught in her earliest lessons on Islam.

"But we don't obey Allah so that we can have a good life in this world," I said. "We obey Him so we can have a good life in the Hereafter."

"But can't I have a good life in both worlds?" she asked, exasperated.

"Yes," I said. "But it's Allah who defines what that looks like for us."

Putting Things Into Perspective

I remember reading a quote by Yasmin Mogahed that really resonated with me: "The secret to happiness is to not make it dependent on that which can be taken away."

But unfortunately, so much of what we're taught about our lives in this world, even from many spiritual teachers and imams, is that we'll be granted worldly happiness and materialistic success if we're "good Muslims." Or that if we just have enough faith, all our wildest dreams will come true. I've even heard advice from fellow Muslim entrepreneurs that equated our income level with the spiritual state of our souls.

"If you think good of Allah, He'll grant you all that you want in this world," they say. "You just have to trust in Him." While I certainly believe in both the power and necessity of thinking good of Allah and of our heart's need to trust in Him, I grow very uncomfortable when these tools for spiritual nourishment and soul purification are taught for the purpose of promising very specific worldly outcomes.

It's not that I believe that we shouldn't strive for worldly success. Quite the opposite. In fact, I personally believe that we need to do a much better job at securing economic independence as Muslims, if for no other reason than we shouldn't be relying so heavily on those outside our faith to sustain our families and communities.

Once during a keynote speech that I gave about increasing our wealth in this world, I shared this advice: *Don't use your belief in the Hereafter as an excuse to settle for failure and helplessness in this world.* When the Prophet (peace and blessings be upon him) and the Companions lived simply, it was because they were generous with their wealth and worldly success, not because they didn't have any. And it certainly wasn't because they shunned working for wealth and success in this world.

I then shared this *ayah* from Qur'an, which has been translated to mean:

> **"But seek, with that (wealth) which Allah has bestowed on you, the home of the Hereafter, and forget not your portion of legal enjoyment in this world. And do good as Allah has been good to you, and seek not mischief in the land. Verily, Allah likes not those who do mischief"**
> (*Al-Qasas,* 28:77).

Thus, it is upon us as believers to strive our level best for the best in this world and the best in the Hereafter, while seeking from this materialistic world that which is blessed and *halaal* for us.

However, as we strive for worldly success, we need to approach this noble goal with a different mindset than we do for ultimate spiritual success in the Hereafter. If we do not, our spiritual lives will suffer tremendously, and we will continuously be confused when things don't turn out the way we expected.

Why We Get So Confused

Here's a reminder I wrote to myself in my personal journal, in hopes of protecting my heart from the unnecessary turmoil that would befall it if I didn't keep this world in proper perspective:

You know why we get so confused? Because we think of success in this world how we should think of success in the Hereafter. Allah promises us very specific rewards in the Hereafter due to our soul work, and we promise *ourselves* very specific rewards in this world due to our *dunya* work.

Relationship advisors share tips that promise long-lasting, loving marriages—or that guarantee *knowing* when someone is right for you. Business gurus share tips that promise having plentiful wealth and a successful business—and that promise ways to be debt-free and relieved from financial struggle forever. Even some spiritual teachers go as far as to tell you that all of this worldly happiness and success is promised to you if you're a "good Muslim."

And to prove they're right, they'll point to the perceived "success" in their own lives or in someone else's—thereby taking credit for God's work by saying these blessings are due to their own efforts.

But the life of this world doesn't work like that.

You cannot gift your *qadar* (God's decree) to someone else, no matter how convinced you are that they should follow in your footsteps to have success, wealth, or a lasting marriage. The result didn't come from you, so someone following your advice won't grant them your life path.

Yes, we can benefit from each other's journeys, experiences and advice, but we cannot duplicate other people's successful results. And we shouldn't even want to. Because we have no idea what trials await our souls and our families if we taste the result of someone else's definition of "success."

There are only two things that every soul is promised in this world: earthly trials and inevitable death. So if you want "foolproof" tips that promise success, then look to divine guidance on how to patiently endure worldly trials and how to gratefully appreciate worldly blessings.

And through this, *bi'idhnillaah*, you'll learn how to attain the only success that really matters in the end: meeting your Rabb in a state of sincere submission and faith, and then finding that He is pleased with you.

2

What Are You Teaching Your Heart?

The Companion Sahl bin Sa'd As-Sa'idi (may Allah be pleased with him) said that a man came to the Prophet (peace and blessings be upon him) and said, "O Messenger of Allah, guide me to such an action which, if I do it, Allah will love me and the people will also love me."

He (peace and blessings be upon him) said, "Have no desire for this world, and Allah will love you; and have no desire for what people possess, and the people will love you" (Ibn Majah).

Prophet Muhammad (peace and blessings be upon him) also said, "Whoever makes the world his most important matter, Allah will confound his affairs and make poverty appear before his eyes and he will not get anything from the world but what has been decreed for him. Whoever makes the Hereafter his most important matter, Allah will settle his affairs and make him content in his heart and the world will come to him although he does not want it" (Sunan Ibn Majah 4105, *Sahih* by Al-Albaani).

Spiritual Gems

When I reflect on the spiritual beauty and soul nourishment in these gems of prophetic advice, I can't help but notice how these directives are in stark contrast to what we are being taught today with regards to securing wealth and material success, even in Muslim circles.

So much of the advice we receive on attaining worldly success is about using the tools of soul purification (such as worship and obedience to Allah) as a means to gain tangible worldly outcomes—like a lasting marriage, plentiful wealth, the perfect body, and so on.

In many cases, this sort of advice stems from us looking at the worldly happiness and success of the disbelievers and hoping to secure the same "happiness" and "success" for ourselves. With this mindset, we study concepts like "the law of attraction" and "channeling the energy of the Universe," and then attach our hearts to these ideologies in order to get what we want in life. Then we seek to make Islamic spirituality align with all of this, while pointing to how Allah promises to answer our supplications and how He is how His servant thinks He is.

We even shame those who remind us to focus on the Hereafter, by painting them as extreme ascetics who shun everything of this world and want to "sit around" in poverty and consider it piety. While there are certainly fringes of Muslims who have this misguided understanding of *zuhd* (spiritual detachment from this world), the issue goes so much deeper than that.

In this, I am not suggesting that we abandon seeking wealth and worldly comforts or happy, long-lasting marriages. Rather we must sincerely ask our hearts: *Are we being honest with ourselves when we link Islamic spirituality to attaining specific worldly results? Is this what our Creator is teaching us? Is this what prophetic guidance is teaching us?*

If our answer is "no" to these last two questions, then this weightier question remains: *Why then are we teaching this to our hearts?*

Which World Is Your Heart Attached To?

To be clear, the problem here isn't that we are relying on Islamic spirituality to attain worldly success. Rather the problem is that we are making this worldly success our starting point and focus in life. While Islamic spirituality definitely includes divine prescriptions for attaining worldly success, all of these means are channeled through the lens of nourishing our souls, pleasing Allah, and placing the Hereafter above this world.

This is so much the case that nearly everything in the Qur'an and prophetic teachings points to this one foundational perspective on worldly success: True success in this world is attached to our willingness to let go of our wealth, worldly statuses, and even our own loved ones, if this is what it takes to save our souls and obey our Creator.

Allah says what has been translated to mean:

"Say, 'If your fathers, your sons, your brothers, your wives, your relatives, wealth which you have obtained, commerce wherein you fear decline, and dwellings with which you are pleased are more beloved to you than Allah and His Messenger and striving in His cause, then wait until Allah executes His command. And Allah does not guide the defiantly disobedient people"
(*At-Tawbah*, 9:24).

What is so profound about this *ayah* is that Allah mentions our attachment to our loved ones and spouses before He even mentions our attachment to our wealth, property, and businesses. This in itself should be a deep lesson to our hearts that even when our religious advice focuses on having success in our family relationships and marriages, this is imbalanced if it is not filtered through an understanding that we might one day need to sacrifice even these relationships to save our souls.

But if our hearts are attached to this world more than the Hereafter, how is this even possible?

3

Be Willing To Let Go Of It All

A couple of years ago, my then twenty-year-old daughter came to me excited about starting her own business. Naturally, as an entrepreneur myself, I was excited for her, and I offered my full support and prayed for her success. And I continue to.

However, I cautioned her:

If Allah blesses you with wealth, be sure not to get too attached to it. Because everything in this world is a trial, even our worldly blessings. Everything we seek or receive in this world should be used as a means of nourishing our souls and securing success for ourselves in the Hereafter.

So keep in mind that anything you love or are granted in this world, Allah will test you with it. This is to see if your heart values that worldly blessing more than you value Allah's Pleasure and the Hereafter. So while it's a tremendous blessing to be granted lots of wealth, if it ever comes to choosing between your soul and your wealth, you must be willing to walk away from it all, if it means protecting your soul.

A Light in the Dark Night

Once, the Companion Abu Dharr Jundub bin Abdullah (may Allah be pleased with him) said: "I advise you to fear Allah and obey Him (with *taqwaa*), and I advise you to adhere to the Qur'an, for it is a light in the dark night and a guidance during the day. So, implement it no matter how much struggle and poverty you have to face.

"If a calamity befalls you, put your wealth forward to protect your religion, and if the calamity continues, put forward your wealth and your life to save your religion [but never risk your religion].

"For the ruined is he whose religion is ruined, and the robbed is he whose religion is taken. And know that there is no poverty after Paradise, and no riches after the Fire" (Adh-Dhahabi, Siyar A'laam an-Nubalaa, 3/174).

God Isn't Handing Out Stickers for Good Behavior

One of the things I remind myself is that we shouldn't look at our worship of Allah like we look at the extrinsic reward system of this world, wherein we're given stickers and rewards for being "good girls and boys."

Getting worldly wealth, success, and happiness isn't a mathematical formula where you input prayer and good deeds and then lots of money or the perfect marriage is the output. Allah is not our personal "servant," bank teller or wish-granter, whose only role in our lives is to give us what we ask or demand from Him.

Viewing our relationship with Allah in this way contradicts true faith and *tawakkul* (sincere trust in Him). And contrary to popular belief, this mindset does *not* reflect thinking good of Him. Rather it's a sign of entitlement and arrogance—and ignoring His divine attribute of being our Rabb, the Master and Owner of our lives.

In truth, Allah owes us nothing in this world. Yet we owe Allah everything—including our very souls and lives. It is we who are His servants and who are obligated to do what He asks and demands of us, not the other way around.

Yes, in this spiritual servitude, we are also granted many of the things we seek and desire of this world. But this is not because it is owed to us. It is because of Allah's Mercy, Generosity and Compassion.

You Get What You Strive For

Allah says what has been translated to mean:

"Whoever should desire the transitory things [of this life], We hasten for him from it what We will to whom We will. Then We have made for him Hell, which he will [enter to] burn, censured and banished. But whoever desires the Hereafter and exerts the effort due to it while he is a believer, it is those whose effort is ever appreciated [by Allah]. To each [category] We extend – to these and to those – from the gift of your Lord. And never has the gift of your Lord been restricted. Look how We have favored [in provision] some of them over others. But the Hereafter is greater in degrees [of difference] and greater in distinction"
(Al-Israa, 17:18-21).

He also says:

"…And whoever desires the reward of this world, We will give him thereof; and whoever desires the reward of the Hereafter, We will give him thereof. And We will reward the grateful"
(Ali 'Imraan, 3:145).

So as we seek the transitory enjoyments of this world, let us strive to be spiritually honest with regards to our ideas of the happiness and success we enjoy during our brief sojourn here—before we are lowered beneath the ground.

4

Motivators Within the Heart

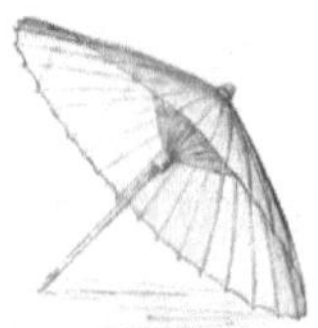

Escaping pain and seeking pleasure are two powerful motivators within the heart. So be alert, dear soul, for when these inclinations are at odds with the needs of your soul.

Pay attention to the pathways in your heart toward love and escaping hurt.

We speak a lot about the importance of self-honesty, but it is rare that we actually look deep inside to learn what this actually means—for us specifically.

When it comes to soul-care, one of the most essential aspects of self-honesty is being keenly aware of your weaknesses and inclination toward sin. However, this is only a starting point. Focusing all your attention on only one pathway to spiritual harm is like looking only one way when crossing a busy intersection. There are numerous pathways that can harm our souls.

And the most dangerous pathway to harm does not always stem from temptation toward sin. It also includes the pathways of seeking our hopes and dreams—especially in pursuit of love, family, and wealth. It also includes the pathways to escaping pain—especially when some aspects of our faith and spiritual practice trigger painful memories from our past.

In guarding these pathways in our hearts, here are some questions we can ask ourselves:

When I think of love or escaping pain, what am I hoping for? What am I seeking? And what am I willing to do to get it? What am I willing to do to keep it?

And what am I not *willing to do?*

How do I protect my soul from the harm that comes from seeking love or escaping pain? And for the sake of my soul, am I willing to sacrifice love? Am I willing to endure pain?

And while seeking what I want in this world, am I allowing my emotions to guide my spirituality, or am I allowing my spirituality to guide my emotions?

5

Where the Grass Is Greener

As I meet more and more people who take credit for God's work in their lives and claim it to be their own—saying their positive mindset and hard work alone "channeled the energy of the Universe" in their favor—I'm growing to appreciate the wisdom in the simple utterance, "*Alhamdulillaah*" (i.e. "All praise and thanks belong to Allah") and in the simple act of *sajdatu-shukr* (prostration for gratefulness), wherein we place our foreheads humbly on the ground and glorify our Creator after something good has happened in our lives.

In moving our tongue in remembrance of our Creator after every *qadar* (good and bad), we are reminded where both the power and praise always belong. And in placing our heads humbly on the ground after receiving good news, we are reminded where we ourselves always belong—in humble remembrance that our highest honor is found in embracing our humility before God, not in claiming our greatness before His creation.

Yes, the ground where you place your head might have "greener grass" than someone else's. But don't assume it's because you put in all the necessary work while they didn't. Your grass is not greener only because you watered it. It's greener because God planted it, thus giving you something to water in the first place. Then He granted you the

knowledge and tools you needed to make that grass grow—
which is more a testimony to His greatness than your work.

We wouldn't have even a patch of dirt to stand on—let
alone grass growing from it—if it weren't for God saying
"Be" and granting it to us.

So before you share how much you watered your grass
and someone else didn't, take a moment to praise and
acknowledge the One who can strip it all from you in the
blink of an eye, like He did with the arrogant man who
owned the beautiful gardens in *Surah Al-Kahf* (18:32-43).

And be careful, lest in boldly declaring your "tools to
success"—whether in amassing wealth or knowledge, or in
having a lasting marriage or strong family ties—you become
like those whom our Creator warns us about in the Qur'an:

> **"Think not that those who exult in what they have
> brought about, and love to be praised for what they
> have not done—never think them [to be] safe from
> punishment [of Allah]..."**
> (*Ali 'Imraan*, 3:188).

And we seek Allah's protection, guidance, and
forgiveness wherever we have forgotten our Creator, or
ourselves.

Yaa Rabb! A Heartful Prayer

*O Allah, we ask You to soften our hearts and place in them
compassion and empathy for all of Your creation—especially for Your
believing servants who are struggling in ways that we cannot
understand or comprehend, and who are battling trials that we have
not been tested with!*

*And O Al-Muhaymin (Granter of Security), Al-Ghaffaar (Ever
Forgiving)! We beg You to protect us from the evil within ourselves,*

and forgive us our sins and faults, both hidden and open, and of what we know and what we don't know!

And O Al-Wahhaab (Bestower of Goodness), Al-Haadee (The One Who Guides)! Remove from our hearts the stains of arrogance, self-praise, and kibr (looking down on others and rejecting the truth)! And O Allah, Al-Kareem (The Most Generous)! We beg You to make every trial You place in our lives, whether in ease or hardship, cause us to draw closer to You in humility, gratitude, and tawakkul (sincere trust in Your plan, guidance, and decree) until we meet You!

Lesson Two
Pain and Pleasure

*"Pain is a fuel for the pleasure, and pleasure is a fuel for the pain.
When something is beneficial or necessary for you, your ultimate
success and pleasure in it depends largely on how patient you are with
the pain and sacrifice that come along with attaining it. When
something is harmful or forbidden for you, the more you indulge in the
fleeting pleasure of it, the more pain you'll suffer in the long run.
Either way, you're going to suffer pain.
Just make sure you choose the fleeting pain, not the fleeting pleasure.
Otherwise, you'll have long-term pain instead of long-term
success and happiness."*
—from the journal of Umm Zakiyyah

6

Is It a Test or a Punishment?

"How do I know if it's a test or a punishment?" This is a question I wondered about for years, and every chance I got, I asked an Islamic teacher or read whatever I could on the issue. Till today, the answer that stays with me is this: You don't.

Ultimately, only Allah knows why He's putting believers through certain trials. Also, a test and a punishment are not mutually exclusive. Both could be happening at once.

All of life is a test for the human being, so everything we experience is meant to direct us back to our purpose: worshipping and serving our Creator. Whether we are experiencing ease or hardship, enjoying the worldly fruit of honest hard work, or suffering the bitter consequences of arrogantly disobeying Allah; we have in each circumstance the opportunity to seek Allah's pleasure, beg His forgiveness, and attain Paradise when we die.

In other words, even if the worst is true—we're being punished for our sins—this in itself isn't "the end of the world." Often, believers experience pain, trials, and punishment on earth so that they are spared from torment for their sins in the Hereafter.

And if the worldly trial—or punishment—is encouraging us to turn to Allah, repent, and improve our spiritual lives;

what practical benefit do we gain from obsessing over whether or not Allah is angry with us?

Unless we are arrogantly seeking to continue disobeying Allah and need a serious reality check, fixating on the question of Allah's anger can become a distraction from our spiritual growth. No matter what is or is not happening in our life (and why), we should be worshipping Allah and seeking His guidance and forgiveness anyway.

And would—or should—knowing whether you are facing a trial or a punishment change this noble focus for you?

7

Allah Owes Us Nothing

It took me months and years of emotional and spiritual healing before my heart could comprehend the profundity and beauty of this basic truth: *Allah owes you nothing.* Whether it is wealth, health, a certain type of marriage, children, or even faith itself; Allah doesn't owe it to you. Thus, feelings of resentment, frustration, and anger regarding your ostensibly "inferior" life station and painful life experiences don't make any sense.

Allah is the Creator of all, so He can do what He pleases, how He pleases, and when He pleases; and He isn't answerable for a single thing He decrees. He can raise the status of some people and lower the status of others—in this world or in the Hereafter—and there is not a single injustice involved, no matter how "imbalanced" these decisions appear to us.

Allah says what has been translated to mean,

"Indeed, Allah will admit those who believe and do righteous deeds to gardens beneath which rivers flow. Indeed, Allah does what He pleases"
(*Al-Hajj*, 22:14).

He says further,

"Indeed, Allah does not do injustice, [even] as much as an atom's weight; while if there is a good deed,

**He multiplies it and gives from Himself
a great reward"**
(*An-Nisaa*, 4:40).

He also says,

**"He is not questioned about what He does, but they
will be questioned"**
(*Al-Anbiyaa'*, 21:23).

The Heart Is the Equalizer

The heart is the great equalizer. This is what I've come to realize about the confusing struggles and apparent "imbalances" in this life, imbalances that once distressed me to the point of nearly losing my faith.

Whether we are looking at the apparent imbalance of power between the privileged and underprivileged, the rich and poor, white people and black people, and even husband and wife, none of this is the point in life. The point is in how our *hearts* comprehend and respond to these "imbalances" during our brief journey to the grave.

When we allow our hearts to imbibe the "imbalances" of life as ultimate representations of the essence of *who we are* (whether in inferiority or superiority in comparison to others), then we've lost sight of the whole purpose in life: purification of the heart and connecting to our Creator.

Irrespective of our "inferior" or "superior" station on earth—and irrespective of how we comprehend that station in relation to the Hereafter—we need to focus on the state of our hearts in this world and its influence on our religious practice if we are to be successful spiritually.

Privileged and Underprivileged

The privileged person whose heart is filled with pride or entitlement due to what they imagine to be their "superior" status (whether due to skin color, gender, bloodline, marriage, nationality, or immense wealth) becomes the *truly* inferior person in front of Allah.

Likewise, the underprivileged person whose heart is filled with resentment or entitlement due to what they imagine to be their "inferior" status (whether due to skin color, gender, bloodline, marriage, nationality, or lacking wealth) too becomes the *truly* inferior person in front of Allah.

And this remains their state unless they repent and work to change their hearts and spiritual practice before they die.

In other words, it doesn't matter where you're standing during your time on this earthly dirt. It matters only how your heart comprehends (and responds to) your temporary stations and experiences on this earthly dirt. Because ultimately, we will all be lowered into this earthly dirt and answer for how we spent our time upon it.

Inequality Is an Illusion

If we sincerely reflect on the transient nature of this world, then we will begin to understand that the apparent "imbalance" of life itself is merely an illusion. Why? Because in His divine wisdom and justice, Allah has made our hearts the great equalizer.

Of course, this doesn't mean that literal inequalities do not exist on earth. Moreover, it doesn't mean that the injustices that humans inflict on each other are figments of our imaginations. It doesn't even mean that there are no significant differences between what Allah bestows on some people and what He bestows on others. In fact, Allah Himself says what has been translated to mean,

"And Allah has favored some of you over others in provision…"
(An-Nahl, 16:71).

He also says,

"To each [category] We extend – to these and to those – from the gift of your Lord. And never has the gift of your Lord been restricted. Look how We have favored [in provision] some of them over others. But the Hereafter is greater in degrees [of difference] and greater in distinction"
(*Al-Israa*,17:20-21).

Thus, what I mean regarding the illusion of imbalance in this world is this: When we process inequalities or imbalances as the *essence* of our life experience, as the essence of who we are, or as a form of divine injustice, then we are measuring our worldly reality based on an illusion.

In other words, it is the ultimate joy or suffering of the human heart that determines the true essence of what we experience in life. Furthermore, it is the ultimate spiritual purity and *taqwaa* of the human heart that determine any person's true superiority in this world.

Those with the purest hearts and sincerest *taqwaa* enjoy both the highest status and the deepest (internal) enjoyment in this world—and in the Hereafter. This is the case even if their ostensible worldly station appears "inferior" or off-putting to other people. Similarly, those with the most resentful and prideful hearts suffer both the lowest status and the most agonizing (internal) suffering in this world and in the Hereafter—even if their ostensible worldly station appears "superior" and appealing to other people.

This is because, truthfully, the greatest enjoyment in this world stems from a heart full of sincere *emaan* and humble *shukr*. Likewise, the deepest suffering in this world stems from a heart full of prideful *kufr*, arrogant entitlement, and bitter ingratitude.

8

Let's Fix Our Hearts

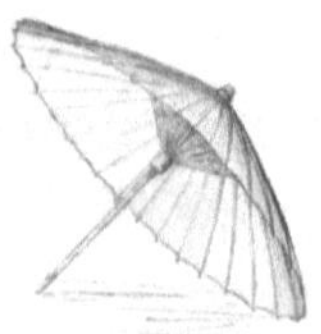

Certainly, the fact that the ultimate reality of life rests in the spiritual state of heart does not mean that those with the purest hearts are protected from suffering the physical and emotional pain that other people endure. In fact, we know from our faith that those with the purest hearts suffer the severest trials in comparison to others.

In a well-known prophetic hadith, the famous Companion Sa'id ibn Abi Waqqas (may Allah be pleased with him) reported, "I said, 'O Messenger of Allah, which people are tested most severely?' The Messenger of Allah, peace and blessings be upon him, said, 'They are the prophets, then the next best, then the next best. A man is tried according to his religion. If he is firm in his religion, his trials will be more severe. If he is weak in his religion, he is tried according to his strength in religion. The servant will continue to be tried until he is left walking upon the earth without any sin" (Sunan al-Tirmidhī 2398, *Sahih* by Al-Albaani).

Likewise, in the Qur'an, Allah repeatedly shares with us powerful imagery and lessons regarding the reality of this world. He lets us know that the tests that befall human souls in this world are for at least four purposes:

(1) warning the sinful and arrogant
(2) encouraging self-reflection in the believers
(3) inspiring repentance in those who wrong their souls
(4) teaching *emaan* and humility to the heedful

However, He informs us that when we turn away from these reminders—thereby rejecting the sincere faith and humility that we are being called to—He removes these painful trials from our lives and replaces them with plentiful worldly enjoyments, excessive pleasure, and a life of ease:

"Verily, We sent (Messengers) to many nations before you. And We seized them with extreme poverty (or loss in wealth) and loss in health with calamities so that they might believe with humility. When Our Torment reached them, why then did they not believe with humility? But their hearts became hardened, and *Shaytaan* (Satan) made fair-seeming to them that which they used to do. So, when they forgot (the warning) with which they had been reminded, We opened to them the gates of every (pleasant) thing, until in the midst of their enjoyment in that which they were given, all of a sudden, We took them to punishment, and lo! They were plunged into destruction with deep regrets and sorrows"
(*Al-An'aam*, 6:42-44).

Everyone Suffers in This World

The reality of this world is that suffering is experienced by every human soul, whether believer or disbeliever. It's just that whatever true believers endure in this world is merely a means to purify their hearts and increase their love and gratefulness toward their Creator. It is also a means of making their *emaan* evident in this world such that this sincere faith will be a testimony for them on the Day of Judgment.

In this regard, Allah in His immeasurable Mercy and Compassion, comforts the hearts of the believers by reassuring them that they are not alone in their suffering (whether physical or emotional), while they are certainly alone in their reward:

"If a wound should touch you, there has already touched the [opposing] people a wound similar to it. And these days [of varying conditions] We alternate among the people so that Allah may make evident those who believe and [may] take to Himself from among you martyrs, and Allah does not like the wrongdoers"
(Ali 'Imraan, 3:140).

So, while sincere believers certainly suffer the most difficult worldly trials, they also have the highest spiritual reward and the deepest worldly pleasure—hearts endowed with spiritual contentment.

Forgetting Our Souls

Unfortunately, despite these repeated reminders and encouragements throughout the Qur'an and prophetic teachings, so many of us forget ourselves until we end up harming our hearts and souls in our confusion, frustration, and despair.

In this, we get so distracted by the details of our life's test or by the pleasure, success, or rights enjoyed by other people that we forget that these details are completely irrelevant in comparison to our higher spiritual goal: purifying the heart.

When this spiritual forgetfulness overtakes our hurting hurts, we can fall into patterns of resentment. I myself fell into this spiritually damaging pattern during a difficult period of my life. During this soul-testing time, I was forced to strive against my *nafs* to overcome this pain, as I discuss in the next section.

Lesson Three
Glimpses of Suffering and Resentment

"And wish not for the things in which Allah has made some of you excel others. For men there is reward for what they have earned, [and likewise] for women there is reward for what they earned. And ask Allah of His Bounty. Surely, Allah is Ever All-Knower of everything."
—Qur'an (*Al-Nisaa*, 4:32)

9

Overcoming the Pain of Resentment

I resented my husband. It wasn't a feeling that I was particularly proud of. But it was there, fermenting in my heart, nonetheless. I had no idea how I got to that dark place, but I couldn't see my way out. In fact, I'm not entirely sure I even saw it as a dark place. It was just life, *my* life.

I tried hard to fight the dark waters of agony and depression. But no matter how many Islamic classes I attended, how much Arabic I learned, and how much Qur'an I studied, recited, and memorized, the dark waters would throttle me and pull me in. At times I feared I would drown in my confusion and pain. But I continued to fight and fight. I fought for my marriage. I fought for my sanity. I fought for my *emaan.*

Until I couldn't fight anymore.

Eventually, I feared I could no longer be Muslim. I *wanted* to be Muslim, but I felt that I just didn't have the mental, emotional, or spiritual capacity anymore. I wondered if this was what it felt like to have the dark veil of disbelief closing over your heart.

"Some people were created as fodder for the Hellfire," a friend of mine said to me one day, "and there's nothing you can do about it."

Her words terrified me.

And I wondered if I was one of them.

Why Do Men Get So Much and Women So Little?

As I felt my heart hardening and the *emaan* leaving my heart, I was overcome with feelings of worthlessness as a woman. I felt that my only value on earth was in servitude to others, particularly men. I felt that I had no value even in front of my Lord, except that I could make a man's life better, happier, or complete.

During this time, I became resentful not only of my husband but also of men in general. And unfortunately, the scholars and imams I turned to for answers didn't help any. In fact, they made matters worse. It seemed like all their teachings centered around placing women's entire value in pleasing their husbands and obeying their leaders.

In other words, I felt like they were telling me that it was only through disappearing myself from existence that I had any meaningful existence in front of Allah.

It would take years of suffering before I was able to finally see myself as a full human being whose value was not dependent on what I could offer men or anyone else. Upon this realization, I penned the following entry in my journal which I share in my book *Pain. From the Journal of Umm Zakiyyah*:

> *You don't need to be someone's wife, mother, or daughter to experience your high status as a woman in Islam. You need to be only the best of yourself—a believer—and Allah raises your ranks by your own merit and deeds.*

You Will Be Tested

Today I know that the terrifying dark period that I went through was just one of the many trials of life. However, at the time, I assumed I was just a bad Muslim whose *qadar* was overtaking her in treading a customized path to Hellfire.

Yes, like nearly every Muslim, I'd heard a great deal about the most momentous battle being our *jihaadul-nafs* (the internal battle of the self against the self), but I'd never dreamed it could reach the dark, debilitating level that I was enduring. Yet in His Book, Allah has made it very clear that not a single one of us will be able to get by on merely claiming to have *emaan*. In the Qur'an, Allah asks what has been translated to mean,

"Do people think that they will be left alone on saying, 'We believe' and that they will not be tested?"
(*Al-'Ankaboot*, 29:2).

He also lets us know that the severe trials in life are not limited to losing our worldly possessions and withstanding harassment and abuse from disbelievers. He tells us that the severe trials of life include being tested within our very selves:

"You shall certainly be tried and tested in your wealth and properties and within your personal selves..."
(*Ali 'Imraan*, 3:186).

So, our only hope in passing these inevitable tests is in focusing on protecting our *emaan*, purifying our hearts, and living a life of *taqwaa*.

10

My Soul Was Losing the Battle

"Do women have the right to exist in marriage?" my husband said. "This is a really important issue to discuss."

It was a rhetorical question, meant to answer itself, meant to point to the absurdity of denying women the right to think for themselves, the right to utilize their God-given talents and intelligence to benefit the world (and themselves), and the right to be seen—*really* seen—by their husbands.

It was meant to imply that marriage for a Muslim woman was never meant to be an indefinite prison sentence, and that being "a righteous wife" was never meant as solitary confinement, a God-issued command for women to be locked away, suffocated by four solitary walls until death.

But it hit me hard, that question. It hit me in a space I didn't even know was wounded.

And I cried.

I didn't mean to. I didn't want to. This was a family business meeting after all. But I should have known this would happen. It was just one in a string of emotional outbursts I'd had in the last several months.

"I'm sorry," I muttered, just as my husband said the same to me.

We were quiet for a moment. I kept my head down.

I didn't like this side of me, this weakness, this vulnerability laid wide open for the world to see. It was like an invisible knife hovering, a blade with a mind and will of its own, threatening to expose my heart before I gave permission for even *myself* to see what lay within.

This was a discomfiting experience, having emotions I couldn't control.

Emotions I Couldn't Control

Muslims don't get depressed, I heard an Islamic teacher say years ago. And like the foolish student of books and classes I was at the time, I thought it was true. So it didn't occur to me that my frequent insomnia, daily migraines, and loss of appetite—and diminished desire to live—could be explained by an emotional wounding of the spirit.

Besides, it was my fault that I was hurting, I told myself. I had no right to my pain. I had no right to my feelings. I had no right to my *self*. "This is what it means to be a good Muslim," I thought. And I was determined to be good.

Forgive and overlook. Forgive and overlook I kept telling my hurting heart. *Don't you want Allah to forgive you?* It never occurred to me that it made no sense to discuss forgiveness before I even fully acknowledged the validity of my pain— and the reality of who'd inflicted it. Otherwise, exactly what was I forgiving, and whom?

But these questions didn't seem to matter in the religious circles that pushed forgiveness more than they compassionately acknowledged hurt, so I didn't allow them to matter to me. Never mind that Allah encouraging forgiveness was never meant as emotional self-flagellation in which you punished yourself for feeling hurt or anger at all. Yet this self-denial and internal suffering was equated with *sabr* and "righteous struggle" in the circles of religiousness that I trusted at the time.

But the truth is, I was depressed, and I couldn't identify it as such, because it didn't exist. At least not for people like me—Muslims who prayed and fasted and read Qur'an every day. And wishing for death…well, I just wanted to go to *Jannah* (sooner rather than later). So that was a good thing, right?

I'm not sure where this idea came from, that Muslims don't get depressed (or in some circles, that *good* Muslims don't get depressed). But it certainly was embraced as divine truth amongst Muslims I'd known since childhood and those I'd befriended later in life. It was repeated so much that it didn't really occur to me to question or doubt it. It was like part of the *shahaadah* itself.

But slowly and surely, I was becoming MIA—missing in action—even in the presence of myself. And then, to add insult to injury, I kept going back to the very people who'd hurt me. And some of them even gloated in my pain.

I didn't know much about toxic relationships at that time, or about the magnetic pull of them when you haven't engaged in honest healing of the self. But healing was an impossibility at the time, because I hadn't yet given myself permission to *feel* the wounds I'd sustained. So how could I heal what I didn't acknowledge existed?

I Never Thought It Would Be Me

When I did the video "I Never Thought It Would Be Me" and then published the book and video series *I Almost Left Islam: How I Reclaimed My Faith*, I was nervous and scared. It was the first time I'd shared something so personal with the world. But I knew I had to do something, say something—to save myself from slipping farther into the abyss.

I didn't want to throw away my soul. I already knew what that meant. But my soul was losing the battle that my suffering spirit had waged against it. And I felt powerless to stop it. I was too weak.

And frankly, a part of me had stopped caring what was right or wrong. But there was a deeper part, the part of my soul that hadn't yet been defeated, that knew I did care.

There were so many emotions going on inside me, not the least of which was toxic shame. There were those who'd looked up to me, even saw me as a spiritual anchor of sorts. How could I face them?

But by then, I was recovering from rock-bottom, and I was slowly rebuilding my existence, *bi'idhnillaah*, after feeling I couldn't be Muslim anymore. I wanted to be, but I couldn't be. At least that's what I'd thought.

By Allah's mercy, I was able to reclaim my faith by telling the truth, my truth, never mind the consequences or negative judgment from people. My soul had been losing the battle against my *nafs*, and I truly believed that speaking openly about my struggles would help my soul ultimately win.

11

A Tough Little Girl

I learned in early childhood to hide how I really felt. In fact, I tried my best to feel nothing at all. When I was four years old, I'd trained myself to go inside myself. It was my hiding place. And it allowed me to put on my tough face, the face of the academic, the "smart girl," who won essay contests and math competitions at public school, and who memorized the most Qur'an at Muslim weekend school—and who was the obedient, "good girl" making her parents proud at home.

There were times that I cried when I was young. But in my memory, it wasn't very often. And it was almost never in front of others, especially not at school. If tears ever escaped in public, it was because there was no space left inside me to contain them anymore. But that was rare, because I spent nearly every waking hour making sure they had ample space to settle within me, and remain unseen.

Nobody cares, so suck it up. That's what I told myself. It was a motto of sorts, and I believed it. And truth be told, I still battle this feeling today, though my heart is slowly but surely embracing the love that the world has to offer, even if only from those few, rare beautiful souls.

During my healing journey, I tried to convince myself that the world wasn't as cold as it felt. But I almost always wore my proverbial heavy coat, face mask, and thick gloves, you know, just in case.

And there I was, years later, at a family business meeting with my coat, mask, and gloves snatched from me, as I was crying over a rhetorical question that wasn't even aimed at me: *Do women have the right to exist in marriage?*

The Few Who Cared

I'm not going to say that no one checked on me or cared for me during my most difficult times. Because there were a few who tried, may Allah bless them. But I was in such a fog that I didn't even know what they were doing and why.

One neighbor would come over whenever my husband traveled, and she'd sleep on the foot of my bed. I just thought she was a really nice person who enjoyed grown-up slumber parties, though I doubt my company was much fun.

Some sisters even tried to understand what was bothering me. But I said I was fine. I didn't understand why they thought anything was bothering me at all. I wasn't offended so much as I was perplexed.

I know today, they knew I'd gone missing. And they were trying to help me find myself.

Lesson Four
Gifts of Wisdom from Pain

vulnerability.
*that's the problem with showing those weak and aching parts
of you that make you human. it gives other humans the license
to point at you, sneeringly, and pretend they don't have human
parts too.*

—excerpt of *even if. bits and pieces from the heart*
of Umm Zakiyyah

12

False Piety Causes Pain

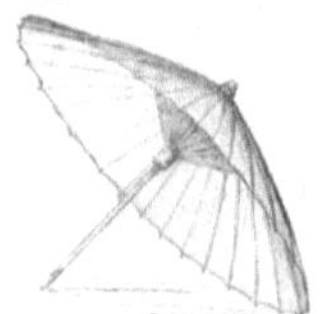

I speak about my life's deepest pain a lot, but let me tell you why: Vulnerable self-honesty is the gateway to our life's deepest pleasures. Just as the closest you get to the Most High is in placing your head on the dirt of the earth, the closest you get to the deepest pleasures of life is in walking honestly and vulnerably through your pain.

Before I embarked on my healing journey, wherein I became honest about my emotional and spiritual wounding, I was living in the shadows of false piety and thinking it to be true faith. False piety is that sterile, rehearsed existence that so many of us learn in the religious books and classes that we imagine teach us all we need to know of spiritual life.

Don't get me wrong. I realize the importance of books and classes, so I'm in no way suggesting that true piety is found in casting them off. What I'm saying is that the essence of true spirituality is the lived experience, not the book or class experience.

By their very nature, books and classes can teach you nothing of experience itself, except the experience of a book or class. Yes, you can learn *about* certain experiences in books or classes. In doing so, you can listen to someone talk about their life or someone else's, or you can read about someone else's life path. But in these contexts, you can learn nothing of your own. This is because experience is its own teacher.

When we equate book and class learning with true spiritual knowledge, we get false piety. And then, tragically, we act out our spiritual lives as if reading from a script.

The Tragedy of False Piety

In false piety, empathy dies, so we fail to see, hear, and *feel* the human hearts of those in front of us. Instead, we observe their speech and behavior and respond according to what we've memorized from the book and class "script."

This is why it is so easy for us to declare that certain people have no love of Allah or Qur'an in their hearts. This is why it is so easy for us to speak so cruelly and dismissively about those who choose plural marriage. This is why it is so easy for us to unilaterally condemn divorce. And this is why it is so easy for us to praise the length of a marriage with no care or concern for what that relationship is doing to the human soul.

This is also why it is so easy for us to openly criticize or mock a woman's efforts in wearing hijab. This is also why it is so easy for us to tell someone to give up a coveted life path or worldly enjoyment "for the sake of Allah"—if it incites *our* spiritual doubt. And this is also why it is so easy for us to then walk away nonchalant, with not the slightest concern or feeling of accountability for how our tongue disrupted the very veins of someone's personal and emotional life.

In this way, false piety wounds friendships, marriages, and even human hearts—sometimes irreparably.

False piety equates emotional impotence with patience, wherein showing no frustration or sadness in response to life's gut-wrenching trials is the mark of a true believer. False piety equates suppressing your pain, smiling when you want to cry, and never speaking about what hurts you, with the highest form of gratefulness.

And false piety equates the silencing of disagreement with anyone in authority—whether a parent, spiritual teacher, or religious scholar—with having *adab* and "showing respect."

13

Heart Over Image

During the time when I was struggling to hold on to my faith, here is something I wrote in my personal journal and subsequently shared in my book, *Pain:*

Oh the script, that religious script,
the one handed to every student of books and classes,
who reads his lines carefully,
then takes the stage,
declaring what is right or wrong in the life of the
unfortunate souls who find themselves the unwitting
audience of their own lives.

It's difficult to put into words all that inspired these cryptic words, and till today, it is not always easy for my own heart to decode them. But in them are so many hidden lessons from the pain and trials of my life, and amongst them is this: At the heart of false piety is the need to uphold a spiritual image over the need to live an authentic spiritual life. Thus, the biggest threat to false piety is the honest, sincere, empathetic human heart.

Becoming Unfettered from False Piety

Though I could not see it at the time, when I sank into the dark waters of spiritual crisis and almost left Islam, I was being unfettered from the doctrine of false piety. This was so that I could begin, for the first time, striving upon an authentic spiritual life. It was as if I was living the inherent negation that begins our testimony of faith, "*Laa ilaaha illaa Allah.*" In this way, my spiritual crisis was the "*Laa ilaaha…*" of my *shahaadah* as a lived experience: I had to give up every definition of piety that I'd falsely equated with faith in Allah before I could come back to Him testifying, "*…illaa Allah.*"

Now I know that vulnerability and honesty are at the heart of true faith, and that they form the very essence of all true love—of God, the self, and others.

So now, I am resting my head on the dirt of the earth and crying out to my Lord about the pain of my heart and soul. This, so that I can draw closer to Him in this life and in the Hereafter, *bi'idhnillaah.*

Because I now know that a book or class cannot give me spiritual life. They can only point me in the right direction so that I can experience it for myself. Yes, I can recite from a prepared script and put on the face of false piety, walking in obligatory happiness and religiosity in front of people. But if your heart is hurting, your heart is hurting. And ignoring it will only make it worse.

If there is anything my life has taught me, it is this: *Pain demands to be addressed, and cries demand to be heard.* So if we are denying our pain and muffling our cries—whether in the name of positivity, *adab*, or gratefulness—we are not walking the path of faith. We are walking the path of denial. And denial will always be at odds with a healthy human heart.

For this reason, if our books and classes teach us that denial and suppression are the essence of spiritual life and we subsequently embrace this as our expression of faith, pain itself will become our life path. Then our spiritual crisis will become a testimony to ourselves and the world that we have yet to learn the true meaning of faith.

14

Unburdening the Hurting Heart

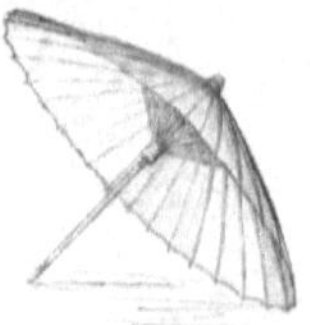

Sadly, there are those who are so afraid of facing their pain that they run from faith altogether, imagining that this will somehow erase from their hearts the agony they're suffering. I almost chose this "easier" path myself. These people live in spiritual numbness while seeking happiness through worldly pleasures sans God. Meanwhile, they never realize that the pain they're running from is merely the gateway to life's deepest pleasures and to imbibing spiritually rejuvenating faith.

The Marathon of Life

Our life in this world is like a customized marathon that has only one requirement for the win: cross the finish line without giving up, no matter how exhausted or distracted you feel in the process—and no matter whom you imagine to be ahead of you. And all of these worldly experiences, struggles, enjoyments and pains are like dancing clowns and hecklers on the sidelines, whose only job is to distract you from seeing and crossing that finish line.

Those whose hearts are focused on the goal—the finish line—do not allow themselves to be unnecessarily distracted by the commotion and shouting on the sidelines, no matter how disturbing or flattering the shouts and jeers.

However, a hurting, wounded heart weighed down by feelings of worthlessness isn't able to even stand or walk properly during its life's marathon. The person's internal wounding makes them too weak and exhausted to even *see* the finish line in front of them.

For this reason, it is incumbent upon all of us who are "walking wounded" to heal our hurting hearts by continuously turning to Allah for help. We must also remove ourselves from relationships and environments that are causing or deepening the wounding of our hearts and souls.

Embracing Humility and Worthiness

Earlier, I discussed a powerful lesson that I learned about the reality of this world: Allah owes us nothing. However, when I was feeling spiritually and emotionally worthless, hearing that Allah owes me nothing would likely have worsened my pain and confusion.

In fact, there were moments during my deepest pain and spiritual confusion that I questioned Allah Himself. *May Allah forgive me and protect me from the soul-damaging darknesses within my nafs.*

But today, because I no longer feel like other people's needs come before my own, and because I no longer feel worthless in front of myself or my Rabb, I can safely and confidently say this (by the Grace and Mercy of Allah): *Even though Allah owes me nothing, I am still a full, worthwhile human being in front of Him.*

In other words, my heart better understands the difference between feeling like you deserve the mercies and blessings of Allah and feeling humbly worthy of them should He gift them to you. This feeling of being worthy of divine gifts is manifested in a life of *shukr* and *emaan*.

In contrast, feeling like you deserve anything in this world incites a sense of entitlement, restless ingratitude, and feelings of frustration or despair whenever things aren't going your way.

In truth, no human being, no matter how righteous or scholarly, *deserves* any favor from Allah, hence the reality that Allah owes us nothing. However, if Allah graces our hearts with *emaan*, then we can become worthy of the mercies and blessings that He showers upon us—despite our ever-present human faults and imperfections.

In fact, this inherent worthiness as a human soul exists irrespective of the mercies and blessings in our lives, and irrespective of the spiritual state of our hearts. This worthiness is the very reason that submission to Allah is a fundamental right of the human soul, and why turning away from submission to Allah is a tremendous *dhulm* to the human soul.

In other words, our hurting hearts become unburdened and our restless souls find peace when we embrace the humility and worthiness found in a life of *emaan* and *shukr*.

15

Knowing Your Worth

It's a lesson that took many years for my heart to understand in a way that was healthy for my soul: My worthiness is neither increased nor decreased based upon what others have, even if it's something I don't have myself, and even if the person has rights over me.

With regards to my status as a wife in marriage, I wrote this note in my journal, and it resonates with my heart more and more each day: *I have a worth that my husband couldn't hope to touch, even if he married three other women besides me. Neither God nor I measure my worth by the actions of a man.*

The Gift of Emotional Freedom

The realization of my inherent worth as a woman in marriage can be likened to the emotional freedom enjoyed by a sincerely generous person who loves to give gifts and charity yet never feels the need to measure what *others* are giving or receiving.

Such freedom comes from a heart that is unburdened with emotional or spiritual wounding that distracts it from its purpose in the human body: to be a source of life. Just like the physical heart exists to be a source of physical life for the human body, the spiritual heart exists to be a source of spiritual life to the human soul.

This is not to say that my heart is spiritually pure or fully healed. It's just to say that my heart has healed *enough* from where it used to be, such that I no longer feel excessively burdened by feelings of worthlessness in front of Allah or other people. For this reason, I can better appreciate that having *emaan* itself is a blessing, not a right that my Lord owes me. And my *emaan* no longer feels like a weighty burden that I begrudgingly owe Allah.

Walking in Dignity

As I embraced more and more emotional freedom during my healing journey, I became more and more aware of my inherent worth as a human soul. This in turn allowed me to become more protective of my emotional and spiritual dignity. As a result, I began to distance myself from unhealthy religious environments and toxic relationships that did not reflect my valuable worth or did not nourish my emotional and spiritual health.

During this time of personal and spiritual growth, I wrote this note in my journal:

> *Know your worth, and act accordingly. This isn't arrogance. It's acknowledging your blessings. Being grateful requires knowing what you are grateful for. You are blessed. So act accordingly—with the dignity, humility and gratefulness that reflects your worth.*

16

Focusing on the Self

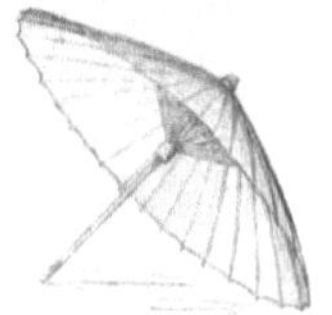

Today I don't care so much about what worldly "privileges" are enjoyed by men and not women, rich people and not poor people, white people and not black people, or even my husband or family and not myself.

So long as no one is being wronged, oppressed, or denied their human rights based on someone's arrogant behavior or perception of worldly privilege, I see these privileges as merely weighty tests in life—many of which I have no desire to carry myself. For with greater gifts comes greater responsibility, and with greater responsibility comes much more to answer for on the Day of Judgment.

Just like I have my own customized "marathon of life," so it is with every other person in this world, even those who enjoy privileges over me.

As for those who restlessly seek the privileges and enjoyments of this world at the price of the Hereafter, Allah says what has been translated to mean:

"Whoever should desire the transitory things [of this life], We hasten for him from it what We will to whom We will. Then We have made for him Hell, which he will [enter to] burn, censured and banished.
But whoever desires the Hereafter and exerts the effort due to it while he is a believer, it is those whose effort

is ever appreciated [by Allah]. To each [category] We
extend – to these and to those – from the gift of your
Lord. And never has the gift of your Lord been
restricted. Look how We have favored [in provision]
some of them over others. But the Hereafter is greater
in degrees [of difference] and greater in distinction."
(*Al-Israa'*, 17:18-21).

He also says,

"…And whoever desires the reward of this world, We
will give him thereof; and whoever desires the reward
of the Hereafter, We will give him thereof. And We will
reward the grateful"
(*Ali 'Imraan*, 3:145).

That the rich and privileged as a group are significantly
less likely than the poor and oppressed to pass the spiritual
tests of life should make these "superior" life stations very
unattractive to us—if we are sincerely focused on purifying
our hearts and embracing a lifestyle of gratefulness.

During this marathon of life, our differences in paths and
responsibilities—or even in privileges and worldly
enjoyments—are not reflective of any "injustice" of Allah or
of His favoring any group over another. They are merely
reflective of Allah's infinite wisdom in knowing exactly what
tests *we* need to focus on what's most important: our hearts.

17

Thank God for Pain:
Ten Things Suffering Taught Me

Shukr. Looking within. Trusting the pain and loss.

As I step into a new phase of healing and striving for self-betterment, these are the things that I'm striving to focus on and implement in my heart and life.

In these past few years, I've worked through so much emotional wounding and spiritual turmoil that it's difficult to even recall at times, the memories are so painful. But Allah brought me through so much, and I learned so much, *alhamdulillaah.*

Here are ten (10) lessons that stay with me from my healing journey:

(1) Growth hurts, a lot. So there's nothing to do but embrace the process, instead of anxiously awaiting the pleasure or relief. If you anxiously await anything without embracing the natural (and necessary) process, even when the pleasure and relief come, they won't feel like pleasure or relief. Instead, they will feel like fear and anxiety, as you are so fixated on escaping pain that you spend times of pleasure and relief frantically fearing that the pain will come back. Thus, you can never genuinely enjoy either the pleasure or relief in your life.

(2) Pain and pleasure are two parts of a whole. You cannot fully experience the latter until you patiently allow the former, without anxious resistance. Allah created things in pairs. Thus, there are things that you cannot have unless you have the other. The pleasure-pain experience is one of those things. We learn this in the sixth pillar of *emaan* (true faith), as famously narrated in the Hadeeth of Jibreel (Gabriel), when the Angel Jibreel came in the form of a man to the Prophet (*sallallaahu'alayhi wa sallam*) and asked him about Islam, *emaan*, and *ihsaan* (worshipping Allah as if you see Him).

When the Prophet mentioned the last pillar of *emaan*, belief in *qadar* (Allah's decree), he went on to specify what this belief entails: accepting the reality of both the *khayr* (good) and the *sharr* (evil) that is destined in our lives (Muslim).

Thus, when we eagerly embrace the pleasure and happiness in life while becoming confused, frustrated, and angry about the pain, then we have a deficiency in our *emaan* that needs to be addressed.

During my own healing journey, this deficiency became painfully apparent to me. Consequently, I realized that I needed to do a lot of soul-work to address this spiritual ailment. And the struggle continues.

(3) Internal battles never cease. They merely change form and intensity, that is all. But they *can* get easier and more peaceful, *bi'idhnillaah*, so long as you have sincere *shukr* (gratefulness) and beautiful *sabr* (patience).

And this in itself is a daily battle and process. So, finding peace as you work through the inevitable internal chaos is the goal.

(4) As you let go of toxic relationships and embrace healthier ones in your life, understand that there will be

those who, due to their own growth, need to let go of you, too. So often we think of toxicity as moving in only one direction, or as rooted only in someone being a corrupt or bad person. However, many times being in a toxic relationship simply means that their flaws are not compatible with ours.

Or, it just means that *our own* unhealed emotional and spiritual wounds make the company of some (though not all) genuinely good people unhealthy for us—even as they are (perhaps) better than we are, in the sight of Allah. In fact, it could be that they incite pain in us for the very reason that they are emotionally and spiritually healthier than we are; however, they just lack the tools to invite us to a better version of ourselves in a non-triggering way.

Therefore, regardless of their honorable spiritual status in front of the Creator, this itself doesn't necessarily mean that they are good companions for us in this world. Because the truth is, some good people simply are not good for *us* specifically. In this, it's helpful to remember that who someone is to Allah and who they are to us are two completely different things. In fact, when distancing ourselves from toxic relationships, we should be concerned with only who someone is to us, as their station in front of Allah is a matter of the *ghayb* that we shouldn't even attempt to delve into.

Nevertheless, it is true that we should love all believers for the sake of Allah. At the same time, loving someone for the sake of Allah doesn't necessarily require making them our closest friend, for example, or trusting them in a business relationship, or marrying them (or even *staying* married to them). You really can love people from afar. Thus, it is completely possible that a believer could be sincere and good, but still be "bad for us" as a close, intimate companion or life partner in this world.

A part of emotional and spiritual maturity is realizing—and fully embracing—that just because we deem a person as "bad for us" doesn't necessarily mean that they are a bad person. And we shouldn't seek to make them out to be. Except in cases of clear evil, oppression, and abuse, there really is no need to come to any conclusion about someone (good or bad) when a relationship ends—except to conclude that they fulfilled the purpose that God decreed for them in our lives. And now it's time to move on.

In other words, our exes (whether friends, business partners, or spouses) are just people—flawed human beings just like we are—whom God simply did not write will be with us on the next part of our journey.

(5) The need to label former friends, companions, and romantic partners (or even estranged family members) as bad people simply because they chose to walk away from us—or because we chose to walk away from them—is often a sign of a serious problem within us. In the secular world, this self-centered labeling of others (based solely on their current or past relationship with us) would be called narcissism. In the spiritual world, it would be called a disease of the heart.

This is because there is only One from whom a broken relationship automatically points to a problem in the person who is no longer connected to them: God Himself.

And we are not God.

(6) It is <u>not</u> true that anyone who is no longer your friend was never a true friend to begin with. This thinking is rooted in the same narcissism and spiritual ailment that I discussed above.

When I discovered the harmful results of this culturally indoctrinated message in my own heart, I asked Allah to remove it from me. And truthfully, I still strive to have its remnants removed from my heart today.

During my healing journey, I discovered that my need to label as "true friends" only those who are dedicated to me—and stand by me no matter what—meant that I was (even though unintentionally) assigning subtle divine attributes to myself. May Allah forgive me. As I discussed above, only God has this high status in *every* person's life. Thus, it is only He who deserves "unconditional" love and dedication, no matter what.

In other words: Someone's unconditional dedication to *us* is not the measure of true friendship. It is only their Creator that they owe such allegiance.

In fact, when there is a break in a friendship bond, it is often the case (in fact, I would venture to say, it is *most often* the case) that you two are just moving in significantly different directions in life. And these diverging directions do not always mean that their path is bad and yours is good (or vice versa). Sometimes the diverging of life paths just means you are no longer compatible as friends.

Believers meet for the sake of Allah, and they part for the sake of Allah. Thus, whether we are meeting someone or parting from someone, particularly a fellow believer, neither circumstance (of building a friendship or dissolving one) has to point to anything inherently bad (or good) in either of us.

(7) It is also <u>not</u> true that if someone truly loves us, they'll stick by us no matter what, even in our darkest days. Yes, if you've been gifted with someone like this, it is indeed a tremendous blessing, and you should thank God for them and strive daily to be grateful for this loving soul companion, as this is indeed true love.

But here's the reality of other types of "true love" (and yes, there are different types): Sometimes people walk away from us *because* they love us. In this case, it was just that their tremendous love for us caused them to constantly put our emotional or spiritual needs before their own—until they were mentally, emotionally, and spiritually depleted themselves.

Thus, the truth regarding "true love" is actually the opposite of what we imagine—and is rooted in our own heart and actions more than someone else's: *If <u>we</u> truly love someone, then we will support them when they do what is best for them, even if that means them choosing their own emotional and spiritual health over a relationship with us.*

(8) Pain and loss are <u>supposed to happen</u> in life. Just like our Lord promises us Paradise in the Hereafter if we believe in Him in this world, He also promises us pain, loss, and severe trials while we live in this world.

In the Qur'an, Allah says what has been translated to mean,

"Do people think that they will be left alone on saying, 'We believe' and that they will not be tested? We did test those before them, and Allah will certainly make known those who are true from those who are liars"
(Al-'Ankaboot, 29:2-3).

He also says,

"You shall certainly be tried and tested in your wealth and properties and within your personal selves…"
(Ali 'Imraan, 3:186).

Yes, our Lord also promises us that He will respond to our supplications and grant us blessings from His bounty. However, it makes no sense to focus on only the promise of abundance, blessings, and Paradise while becoming frustrated, angry, and confused when He fulfills the *other part* of this same promise.

While I was struggling emotionally and spiritually, this was a difficult lesson for my heart and soul to embrace, even after my mind had fully accepted that suffering pain and loss is just a natural part of life, and a fulfillment of my Lord's divine promise.

(9) Worldly success does not equal spiritual success. This lesson might seem obvious because we all "know" it. But what makes this lesson resonate with me so much is that during my healing journey, I realized that some of my emotional pain and spiritual turmoil was the result of my heart not understanding why I wasn't achieving certain tangible worldly results, despite what I felt were my best efforts in constant worship, *du'aa* (prayerful supplication) and obedience to Allah.

Whether it was in my personal relationships or business ventures, or in some of my disappointing experiences with the wider Muslim community, I began to realize that I was expecting my (*inshaaAllah*) sincere spirituality to give me enjoyable, tangible worldly results. Thus, my emotional and spiritual pain were only exacerbated.

Uncovering the truth beneath this pain taught me that there is a huge difference between knowledge and acceptance in the mind, and knowledge and acceptance in the heart. Yes, mentally, I knew that worldly success and spiritual success don't necessarily go hand in hand (and in fact often *don't* for true believers). Yet still, my heart was aching in trying to understand why I wasn't getting the worldly results I so badly wanted and was praying for. When I realized the disconnect, I realized that I had some serious spiritual diseases of the heart to work on, and that was a heavy, difficult realization for me.

As I applied this weighty realization to understanding my unhealed wounds, this honest self-reflection inspired this entry in my personal journal: *What the head knows and what the heart experiences are two different things: Correct knowledge is not difficult to attain, but a spiritually healthy heart? That's a lifelong process.*

(10) Last, and certainly not least: **If you genuinely want to be spiritually healthy, then you need to nourish your heart and soul with at least the <u>minimum</u> amount of attention that you care for your physical body and environment.** Thus, praying the five obligatory prayers on time every day, and reading and reflecting on Qur'an *every day* are just as essential to your spiritual health as having water and food, as well as a clean body and home environment, is to your physical health.

Moreover, just as is the case in our physical world, it doesn't matter how you *feel* about having to, each day, eat food, drink water, and clean yourself and your environment; if you want to be alive and at least minimally well, then it must be done. Similarly, if you want your spiritual heart to be alive and at least minimally well, then the necessary daily spiritual work must be done, irrespective of how you feel about doing it.

In other words, you do what needs to be done because it needs to be done, not because you're always motivated (or happy) to do it. The reality is that you need to be physically clean and nourished, and you need to be spiritually clean and nourished. So there's nothing to do, except the work this cleanliness and nourishment requires.

Nevertheless, there will inevitably be times that you have trouble keeping up with this daily cleanliness and nourishment. Thus, when (not if) this happens, we should ask for help. Yes, there are people who can help us through spiritual difficulties—sometimes. But it is only Allah who will (and can) *always* be there.

So, as we strive to keep up with our daily spiritual purification and nourishment, let us remember that we don't have to do it alone. This is what I reminded myself during my lowest points.

Yes, the reality is, we *will* feel empty and distant from Allah at times. But that doesn't mean we should just give up and assume we are bad people. It only means that Allah, in His infinite mercy and wisdom, wants us to enter His Paradise, *bi'idhnillaah*, so He is showing us the signs that we need to get there. And those signs are that it is time to move closer to Him and beg His help.

As the saying goes, "If you feel distant from Allah, it is only you who moved." Thus, it is you who needs to return to Him; and He will then shower you with His Mercy and Blessings for even the slightest movement in His direction.

So let's get moving, I told myself during those days when I felt like giving up. *Allah is always ready to accept you, no matter how difficult it is to accept yourself.*

And I still tell myself this today.

These are just ten of many lessons that working through my emotional and spiritual suffering taught me. And truthfully, I don't think I would have learned these essential life lessons without the pain.

That is why I, till today, I strive to thank Allah for the pain.

Lesson Five
Prideful, Struggling Hearts

"The only way to get through this life is by being honest with ourselves about ourselves. The beautiful, the troubling, the ugly and heartbreaking. It's all part of you. There isn't a disease of the heart that you aren't susceptible to—and there isn't a purity of heart that you aren't inclined to. And there isn't a lowliness that is impossible for you to sink to—and there isn't a spiritual height that God cannot grant you."
—excerpt of *Pain. From the Journal of Umm Zakiyyah*

18

Is Your Pride Inspiring Harm?

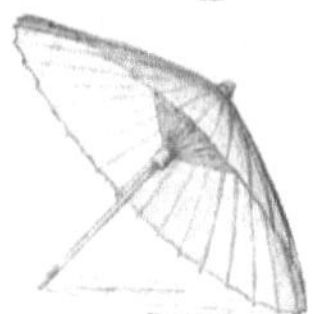

"I don't spend a single moment of my life worried about what will happen to me in the *grave*," the spiritual leader told me indignantly, uttering this last word in disgust. This was his angry response to me telling him that I was striving to live my life in a way that prepared me to have my soul taken as a believer so that I could answer correctly the questions in the grave and be protected from its torment.

I had explained this spiritual goal to him after he insisted that I had a personal responsibility to blindly follow the community imam and spiritual teacher whom he insisted was sent by Allah as mercy and a guide to the African-American people specifically and as a "light of humanity" to the world generally. He told me that in following without question this spiritual teacher, whom He said was taught directly by Allah, I (and my people) would be granted personal, financial, and political success on earth.

"It's the White people's Christian church that fed that 'pie in the sky' mentality to Black people," he said. "But this was just so we'd humbly wait for our heaven in another world while White people enjoyed theirs right here on earth."

However true that may be, I told him, my ultimate goal was to enjoy that very Heaven and "pie in the sky" in the

Hereafter, which so many of my people had desperately longed for as they suffered century after century on earth.

"But we can have the best in both worlds," I explained. "So, I don't see why I have to sacrifice focusing on the Hereafter while seeking personal, financial, and political success on earth."

I also told him that I didn't understand why it was necessary for me to turn away from the teachings of Prophet Muhammad (peace and blessings be upon him) and follow his imam blindly in order to enjoy that worldly success.

Listening to this, he became enraged. And now, because it was clear to him that I was not going to follow without question any human being other than the Prophet, he declared me crazy and arrogant. He then promised to let the world know just how misguided and terrible I was as a person. In this, it was apparent that he imagined he was doing this for some greater good and "higher cause" to benefit our people.

Lost Souls Seeking Success on Earth

Here's what my experience with the spiritual leader taught me: When we don't properly understand (and fulfill) our spiritual obligation to our Merciful Creator on earth, we fail in our duty to our souls—even when we are in the midst of furthering what we imagine to be a good cause in this world. For this reason, it is inevitable that we will also fail in our duty to our fellow brothers and sisters in faith and humanity.

This two-pronged failure is manifested in the *kibr* we exhibit when we rejoice in our own "worldly garden" of community work, political activism, and religious knowledge. Meanwhile, our self-righteous conviction leads us to harass, humiliate, and even slander anyone we feel isn't "stepping up" like we feel they should.

All the while, we are unaware that in our feeling superior to others and demanding they "step up" in how *we* say they should, we are failing to "step up" to the spiritual work that our own souls need.

Signs of Spiritual Self-Abandonment

Whenever our internal spiritual work is lacking or abandoned, we often resort to harassment and cruelty in guilting others into doing what we feel they should. This often takes the form of emotional or spiritual manipulation, slander, casting suspicion on the intentions of others, vilifying the permissible choices of others, public humiliation (often via social media), or full-fledged emotional, verbal, or spiritual abuse.

If we imagine ourselves to be activists for positive change while doing this, we might label our spiritual self-abandonment and cruelty as "standing up for justice." If we imagine ourselves to be righting some wrong in the community or in the personal lives of Muslims, we might label our spiritual self-abandonment and cruelty as "removing an evil with our hands or tongues" or "commanding the good and forbidding the evil."

Regarding the case of assigning ourselves as positive change agents, if we are not careful, our toxic self-righteousness can morph into open sin and sometimes *kufr*. In this spiritually destructive path, we shift from wronging innocent believers to directly opposing the guidance of the Qur'an and Prophet Muhammad (peace and blessings be upon him). This happens when in the midst of righting some perceived wrong, we introduce new behavior codes that replace the ones already gifted to us by Allah through His Book and the prophetic wisdom.

Beware of Pride in Your Heart

When we think of the destructive sin of *kibr*, we so often think of obvious examples like that of an arrogant *faasiq* looking down on practicing Muslims, or Iblis refusing to prostrate to Adam (peace be upon him). However, we rarely reflect on how sinful pride will manifest in our own lives, especially if we think of ourselves as "conscious" citizens or activists calling to social, political, or religious improvement. In reflecting on the dangers of *kibr* overtaking our hearts while we are unaware, I wrote this note in my journal:

Pride will not introduce itself to you or warn you that it's about to destroy your life and heart. It will come cloaked in whatever "good cause" is closest to your heart. If you feel you've been wronged or stripped of something that rightly belongs to you, it will come as your "voice of reason" in demanding what's rightly yours—as it did with Iblis before you.

Be careful. Inflexible conviction in matters that permit, or even demand, flexibility is often a sign that it has settled in your heart.

Pride is the disease that turned the honored Iblis (who was worshipping Allah alongside angels), into the worst devil to ever walk the earth—and it is same sin that can reduce the greatest worshippers, most righteous believers, and celebrated scholars of this faith into the most arrogant, tyrannical people on earth.

Yes, this seemingly simple turning of the heart can cause that much damage.

Be careful.

The only way to protect your heart from pride is to fortify it against itself. And this fortification can only be achieved by constantly turning your heart over to the only One who can protect it from itself.

19

Worshipping Our Desires

"The Prophet is dead, and our imam is alive!" the spiritual leader told me one day, hoping to appeal to me to finally abandon the "misguidance" of following an Arab man from centuries ago. He told me that I was foolish for following an "outdated" version of Islam while Allah had given us (through the community imam and spiritual teacher) a better form of Islam. He said that our imam's version of Islam was more updated and relevant to modern times and more specific to the unique circumstances of African-American people.

Often when I share pieces of my interactions with this spiritual leader, Muslims are shocked and immediately declare that this man is crazy, misguided, and foolish himself. While I do understand this sentiment, what I find most profound is that we don't see the parallels in how we ourselves are essentially making the same arguments whenever we conveniently adjust or reject the Qur'an and prophetic teachings ourselves for the purpose of seeking our own personal, social, and political success on earth. But since we cloak our arguments in more "spiritually appropriate" language, we imagine that we are not as spiritually deceived or misguided as this spiritual leader.

For example, when we introduce or support manmade behavior codes that forbid what Allah has made lawful or permit what Allah has prohibited, we too imagine we are doing this for a greater good. Yet it is well-known that this approach to Islam is *kufr* (disbelief) and *shirk* (assigning to creation rights that belong to Allah exclusively).

Allah says what has been translated to mean, **"They have taken their rabbis and monks as lords besides Allah"** (*At-Tawbah*, 9:31). When 'Adee ibn Haatim (may Allah be pleased with him), a Companion who'd converted to Islam from Christianity, heard this *ayah*, he said, "We didn't worship them."

The Prophet (peace and blessings be upon him) then responded, "Did they not make *haraam* what Allah had made *halaal* and you made it *haraam* [too]? And did they not make *halaal* what Allah had made *haraam*, and you made it *halaal* [too]?" 'Adee replied, "Certainly." The Prophet, *sallallaahu'alayhi wa sallam*, said, "That was how you worshipped them" (Al-Tirmidhi).

We Want What We Want

Arguably, amongst Muslims, the most widely accepted circumstance of introducing new rules into the *deen* of Allah is found in the context of love and marriage. This is where we enthusiastically support manmade behavior codes that (allegedly) promise a desirable outcome in marriage or that protect us from an undesirable outcome in marriage. An example of this is teaching that plural marriage is forbidden in modern times, or that the marriage between a man and his former mistress is invalid, or that any plural marriage that occurred without the first wife giving her enthusiastic consent is null and void.

I imagine that the circumstance of love and marriage is the most widely accepted context of changing the *deen* because it appeals to what the human soul desires most in this world—lasting, intimate companionship with a person they love. And truly, for so many children Adam, we would do almost anything for love, even if it means sacrificing our souls in its pursuit.

In the Qur'an, Allah says what has been translated to mean, **"Have you seen the one who takes as his *ilah* (object of worship) his own vain desires?"** (*Al-Jaathiyah*, 45:23).

However, in most cases, if we identify as practicing Muslims, we don't consciously and deliberately worship our *nafs*. We just find a way to convince our hearts that what we are doing is allowed in Islam, is blessed by Allah, or offers some "greater good" that our unique circumstance demands or permits. This mindset removes the emotional pain of either guilt or feeling accountable for our wrongdoing.

It also removes the possibility of realizing that in this moment, we are little different from the spiritual leader who said outright that we should abandon the "outdated" teachings of Prophet Muhammad (peace and blessings be upon him) in favor of a "better version" of Islam.

20

You Are Not God

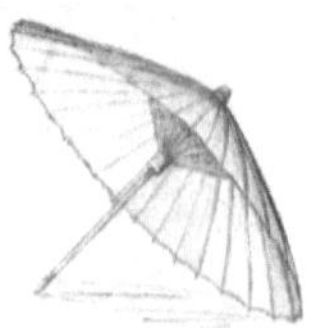

One day, in reflecting on the widespread tendency of Muslims to accept changes in the religion when they appeal to our deepest desires for a specific outcome in love and marriage (and then get upset with whoever reminds us to fear Allah), I wrote this reflection in my journal and shared it on my social media:

Islam means sincere, humble submission to the guidance of God.

Read that again. Then teach it to your heart.

When we begin to introduce our own manmade codes of behavior and defend our "honor codes" by pointing to the bad behavior of Muslim men and women, we're missing the point.

The point isn't that there is something inherently "Islamic" in an older woman marrying a younger man, or an older man marrying a younger woman, or anyone marrying the ex-spouse of a friend or family member, or a woman choosing polygyny, or a repentant man marrying his repentant mistress—or a man marrying the ex-wife of his adopted son (as the Prophet, peace be upon him, himself did).

The point is this and this alone, so listen carefully: You. Are. Not. God.

God is the *only one* with the authority to implement codes of "honor" and moral behavior in this world. And when we begin to attach honor and morality to our own behavior codes, and then slander and harass believers who don't live up to them, then we are setting up ourselves as rivals to God.

And that is no small matter.

This is especially the case when our honor codes are in areas that our Creator has already given us very specific guidelines—such as who can or cannot marry whom, or regarding whose marriage is or is not valid.

Allah and Allah alone is Al-Hakam, The Judge.

If you want to take your chances with facing Al-Hakam on the Day of Judgment with your manmade honor codes—which forbid what He has allowed and allow what He has forbidden—feel free. But I seek refuge in Allah from coming anywhere near *shirk* (the only unforgivable sin), especially if it involves worshipping myself and my feelings and calling others to join in.

So no, there is nothing inherently "Islamic" in one marriage choice over another, and no one is compelled to be in a marriage they dislike. But by Allah, there is something deeply un-Islamic and sinful in saying that any two people that Al-Hakam has made *halaal* for each other, should be forbidden from being together or shamed and slandered for choosing one of the mercies of their Lord.

As for your imagination that these men and women have corrupt intentions in choosing marriages you dislike, you'd do much better to focus on your own corrupt intentions—by assigning the role of Judge and Lawgiver to yourself.

In the Qur'an, the True Judge and Lawgiver tells us:

"It is not for a believer, man or woman, when Allah and His Messenger have decreed a matter that they should have any option in their decision. And whoever

**disobeys Allah and His Messenger, he has indeed
strayed in a plain error"**
(Al-Ahzaab, 33:36).

May Allah protect us from opposing His divine guidance and the prophetic teachings, and may He protect us from using our tongues in this world in a way that would deny us Paradise in the Hereafter.

21

Supporting Dhulm for a Greater Good

When our *kibr* morphs into blatant spiritual transgressions—like those of the spiritual leader openly rejecting the prophetic teachings or of Muslims introducing manmade behavior codes to replace Allah's—it almost always happens under the guise of a good cause. It also almost always happens under the guise of averting some greater harm or opposing some worldly *dhulm* (wrongdoing or injustice).

We can clearly see this form of spiritual self-deception in the example of changing the rules of our religion for the purpose of guaranteeing a certain outcome in our marriages. In almost every case of introducing a new behavior code, our spiritual wrongdoing is defended by pointing to the personal wrongdoing of someone else. But we claim that *our* wrongdoing is for the greater good while *theirs* is for some "selfish goal" like following their desires or mistreating women.

However, when we are fixated on securing (or stopping) a certain worldly outcome that is in front of our eyes while casting the teachings of Allah to the side to attain it, we are suffering from emotional and spiritual myopia. This shortsightedness allows us to see very clearly the good outcome we are (allegedly) guaranteeing with our new rule, or the bad outcome we are (allegedly) preventing.

In this, our blindness to the true greater good—i.e. the greater good as defined by Allah—prevents us from seeing the greater harm that will occur to human lives and souls in the long run when we convince ourselves (and others) that the guidance of Allah is disposable whenever it doesn't fit into what we want for ourselves or our lives today.

Consequently, we are failing to realize this weighty spiritual reality regarding achieving some worldly good or opposing some worldly evil: In Islam, we already have a system of rooting out *dhulm* (wrongdoing and oppression). This divinely mandated system not only preserves the *deen* of Allah but is also an essential part of it.

So, if we are unable (or unwilling) to preserve the rules and guidelines of Allah when responding to *dhulm*, then understand this: All we're doing is just introducing one type of *dhulm* to replace another. And in the end, it just becomes yet another type of *dhulm* that Allah obligates us to root out and oppose.

22

Allah Should Submit To Us?

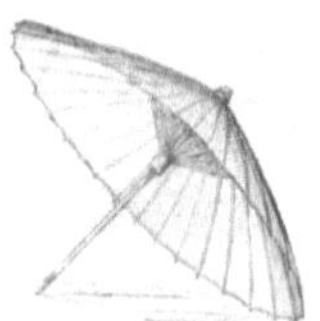

In the spiritually harmful mental space of fighting one type of *dhulm* by introducing (or supporting) another, we are almost always convinced that our intentions are good and that our proposed solutions are necessary, balanced, and compassionate. Even more so, we are often convinced that our newly proposed system of *dhulm* (i.e. our new behavior code that replaces Allah's) represents some "greater good" for ourselves or the believers on earth.

To understand how this happens in real life, think on all the "good reasons" you've heard to outlaw polygyny in modern times, to obligate the enthusiastic consent of the first wife before polygyny can occur, to prevent an older man from marrying a much younger woman, to invalidate the marriage of a former mistress to the married man with whom she committed *zina*, or to slander and humiliate anyone who marries the ex-spouse of a friend or family member.

In each of these new behavior codes, you'll find some argument pointing to a "greater good" that (allegedly) occurs when we replace Allah's laws with those that are "better" or "more honorable" in our personal lives. Unfortunately, the root of this misguided logic is almost always *kibr* or *ghuroor*—that spiritually destructive pride or self-deception that sends so many sincere, well-meaning souls astray. Meanwhile, these "good Muslims" imagine they are acquiring good deeds and implementing some higher good for people on earth.

In the Qur'an, Allah says what has been translated to mean,

"Say, 'Shall We tell you of those who lose most in respect of their deeds? Those whose efforts have been wasted in this life, while they thought they were acquiring good by their deeds"
(*Al-Kahf*, 18:103-104).

In reflecting on the weightiness of this spiritual loss, the sincere believer would strive his or her level best to stay far away from anything that would cause the worst loss in the Hereafter. *May Allah protect us and guide us upon the right path.*

Are We Teaching Allah?

When we convince ourselves of the absolute necessity and wisdom of our personally devised behavior codes, one of two things is usually occurring: We are restricting the mercies that Allah has granted His servants on earth, or we are transgressing the clear limits already set by Allah. In this path of self-deception, we are not only falling into *kibr* and *ghuroor*, but we are also implying that Allah Himself needs to be a student of our interpretations and teachings of Islam instead of the other way around.

Yet in the Qur'an, Allah says what has been translated to mean,

"Say, 'Will you inform Allah about your religion? While Allah knows all that is in the heavens and all that is in the earth, and Allah is All-Aware of everything'"
(*Al-Hujuraat*, 49:16).

23

Protecting People from Allah's Guidance?

"Islam needs to be reformed," the woman said to me. She then told me that the teachings of the Qur'an and the prophetic Sunnah are inherently harmful to people's lives. She also said that these religious teachings guarantee widespread *dhulm* and destruction wherever they are implemented as a foundation of a society. She explained that, for this reason, she herself rejects any spiritual understanding or practice of Islam that is rooted in the actual life of the Prophet (peace and blessings be upon him) and his Companions.

Undoubtedly, this ideology is just another branch of the widely accepted Muslim mentality that introduces or supports new behavior codes for "the greater good" or for rooting out some *dhulm* on earth.

Allah's Rules Cause Harm?

When we introduce or support new behavior codes in hopes of securing a certain worldly outcome for ourselves, we are implying that the teachings of Allah need to be reformed. Thus, as it pertains to the "urgent" issue at hand, we are viewing the divine guidance of the Qur'an and prophetic teachings as either no longer applicable in our times or as insufficient, harmful, or irrelevant to the dire problem we are addressing. Amazingly, we believe this even if the very problem that concerns us is addressed directly in the Qur'an and prophetic teachings themselves.

When we approach a worldly problem in this way, here is the reality of what is happening within us: Deep in our hearts, we sincerely believe that we must protect the believers from the harm that will come to their lives if they follow the guidance of Allah and the prophetic teachings on this issue. Then we proceed to solve the problem ourselves by introducing our (allegedly) wiser and more superior behavior codes that are (allegedly) more relevant and appropriate to the circumstance at hand.

In this, we genuinely imagine (even if only subconsciously) that there is some inherent harm in the divine guidance on this issue and that only *our* solution will protect people from this harm—harm that (allegedly) comes from Allah's rules themselves (*and we ask Allah's protection from this misguided thinking*).

Naturally, this aspect of our spiritual self-deception is often buried deep in our subconscious and is thus unknown to us directly. However, the most glaring sign of this *ghuroor* is that we are introducing the behavior codes themselves— while we have the Book of Allah and prophetic teachings in our hands. And this contradictory reality alone makes us fully accountable for our words and actions, irrespective of whatever unknown beliefs are driving them.

Embracing Emotionalism Over Spirituality

Another glaring sign of this *ghuroor* is that in our spiritual ignorance and emotional immaturity, we use this misguided logic: We look at what will happen to someone if they follow the guidance of Allah or the prophetic teachings on a given issue or in a specific circumstance (for example, living in polygyny), then we equate any resulting worldly loss, painful sacrifice, or emotional pain with them suffering unnecessary harm or *dhulm* in this world. Then we assign ourselves as their savior by introducing the *deen* of emotionalism—in this case hedonism—to replace the *deen* of Allah.

In this, we imagine that attaining perpetual pleasure and happiness in our personal and spiritual lives should take precedence over patient sacrifice in the path of submitting to Allah. Consequently, we genuinely imagine that we are introducing some "greater good" to the lives of Muslims by showing them a path to avoiding emotional pain. Or by showing them a path to (allegedly) guaranteeing a pleasurable outcome that they desire.

However, in this moment of introducing our own behavior codes, which (allegedly) guarantee for people some "greater good" during their brief sojourn in this *dunya*, we are failing to understand that *good* and *pleasure* are not synonyms in front of Allah. In the Qur'an, Allah says what has been translated to mean,

> **"…But perhaps you hate a thing and it is good for you; and perhaps you love a thing and it is bad for you. And Allah knows, while you know not"**
> (*Al-Baqarah*, 2:216).

Moreover, when we introduce our own rules in the case of any "distasteful" circumstance of marriage, for example, we are ignoring the fact that Allah has already given His servants the merciful option of divorce should any marital trial prove too much for them emotionally or spiritually.

Pain Is a Part of Life

At the same time, it is undeniable that it is emotionally painful and difficult to submit to certain distasteful realities like letting go of a beloved (yet toxic) relationship; giving up a harmful (yet beloved) career path; losing valued wealth or status; getting a divorce; or living in an undesirable marital circumstance like polygyny (or monogamy, if we desire otherwise). However, sometimes being required to patiently endure what is extremely unpleasant to us in this world is required by Allah. Or sometimes it is, at the very least, best for our specific circumstances and spiritual path, even if it's not obligatory upon us in our faith.

Furthermore, when it comes to the trials of this world, the reality is this: Sometimes emotional pain is simply unavoidable no matter which path we choose. It's just a matter of which type of emotional pain is healthier for our lives and souls in the long run. (For example: Polygyny or divorce? Unwanted monogamy or emotionally taxing polygyny? An undesirable marriage partner or remaining single?)

For this reason, the believer who is spiritually healthy and emotionally mature understands that in the end, it makes no sense to consistently seek perpetual pleasure and happiness in every moment of our lives. Moreover, the believer understands that something can be genuinely hateful to us at the moment we are being tested with it, yet this circumstance could actually be good or necessary for the betterment of our souls in front of Allah.

Therefore, for the believing soul, there is *never* a need to introduce new behavior codes that forbid any permissible life path that is among the many mercies of Allah, as found in the Qur'an and prophetic teachings. Likewise, there is never a need to introduce new behavior codes that permit ourselves (or others) to transgress the boundaries set by Allah, no matter how much we imagine our new approach is for "the greater good."

Lesson Six
Humility and Self-Correction

"It requires a deep level of sincerity and humility to mess up, sin, or do an embarrassing wrong, yet you get back up and say in front of Allah and the people, 'I was wrong, and I beg Allah's forgiveness for that.'"
—from the journal of Umm Zakiyyah

24

Family Isn't the Foundation of Society

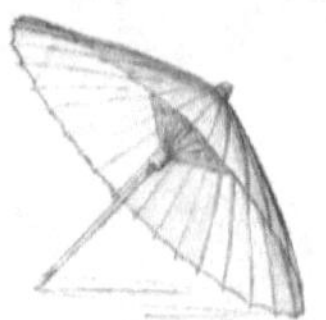

"I don't agree with you getting a divorce," a woman told me after she learned that I was leaving my marriage of over seventeen years to a "good man." In her mind, like in the minds of so many Muslims who mean well but cause so much harm with their religious narcissism, she felt completely justified in standing on the outskirts of my life and telling me what I should or should not do for my soul. For whatever reason, this woman felt she had the right to speak freely about an intimate private decision that she knew little to nothing about. And I hadn't even asked her opinion. I barely knew her.

It didn't matter that I had prayed for *years* about this decision, that I had made *Istikhaarah* multiple times, and that I had sought advice from those who knew my situation much better than she did. In her mind, I was wrong to get a divorce, and she proceeded to go into a long explanation, which could be summarized into a single sentence: *Allah doesn't like divorce, so if you're married to a "good man," then your family should be preserved, no matter what.*

The only exception she allowed—like so many others who created similar behavior codes aimed at governing and micromanaging other people's relationship decisions—was in the case of suffering abuse at the hands of a "bad man."

In witnessing one too many times the continuous habit of so many Muslims speaking with conviction regarding other people's private lives, I once reminded a fellow Muslim of this prophetic hadith: "Part of the perfection of a person's Islam is his leaving that which does not concern him." (Tirmidhi and others; *hasan*).

She immediately retorted, "This *does* concern me." Then she went on to explain how family is the foundation of the community and whatever happens in people's household affects everyone in the community. "Their private life *is* my concern," she said, "because I care about them and I care about the community."

As I listened to how craftily her mind had turned *dhulm* into a good deed, I wondered if we genuinely imagined that we wouldn't be called to account on the Day of Judgment for how we used our tongues or for how many lives and souls we harmed, so long as we could argue that we were harming them for their own good.

Our Spiritual Hypocrisy

In my novel, *His Other Wife*, I share this fictional interaction between two characters that highlights a very real issue:

"Why do we do that?" she asked him one day. "Why do we put rules on ourselves that Allah doesn't? If Allah hates divorce, He hates even more for us to destroy our lives and souls," she said. "And that doesn't only happen when you're married to a monster."

O Allah, the Istikhaarah prayer said, *if you know this situation to be bad for me with regards to my religion, my life and my welfare in the life to come, then distance it from me, and distance me from it…*

"Does the *du'aa* say, 'O Allah, if you know this person to be abusive and horrible'?" she asked rhetorically. "Then we shouldn't be saying it to ourselves when deciding what to do."

"Divorce doesn't have to be tragic," he remembered hearing a relationship expert say during a television interview. *"I'm still not sure why we prefer to believe it must be,"* she'd said, *"especially when there are so many more tragic stories from the homes of two people who would never even consider divorce."*

It's terrifying how confident we are in introducing our own behavior codes and casting aside the Qur'an and prophetic teachings whenever we feel that *our* guidance brings the greater good. Then we turn to the guidance of Allah and His Messenger (peace and blessings be upon him) only when we feel it will work in our favor. Otherwise, we view it as culturally irrelevant or impossible to apply in modern times. This ideology is highlighted in this scene of *His Other Wife* as two characters discuss the topic of plural marriage:

"I just find it interesting that it's only polygamy that brings out our desire for human perfection," Reem said. "But why not advocate for childless marriages since you'll never be the perfect parent? Why not advocate for the lowest possible salary since you might overspend? Why not live in a small, furniture-less house and never buy brand names since they're beyond your needs? We know we're going to be asked about all of this on the Day of Judgment, but it doesn't make us run the other way."

Aliyah nodded thoughtfully but didn't respond.

"All I'm saying is," Reem said, "be honest with yourself. If men need to leave polygamy alone because they can't be completely just, then we need to leave alone having children and nice things since we can't be completely just either."

"But don't you think mistreating another human being is worse than something that can harm only you?" Aliyah said.

"And don't you think helping another human being is better than something that can benefit only you?" Reem countered.

Aliyah coughed laughter. "I don't think the men of today care about helping women."

Reem frowned. "Anyway, Allah didn't say men will mistreat their wives," she said. "He said they won't be able to be fully just no matter how hard they try. And when you study the *tafseer*, this is mainly talking about what's in a man's heart, not his outward actions. The Prophet, *sallallaahu'alayhi wa sallam*, never mistreated his wives, but he loved Ayesha most."

Aliyah nodded thoughtfully. "But can we really compare men of today to the Prophet, peace be upon him?"

Reem walked over to the foyer and slipped on her shoes. "Honestly," she said, exhaustion in her tone, "I hate when people say that. When we think Islam favors monogamy over polygamy, we tell people to follow the Sunnah. But when we realize we're wrong, we say it's impossible to follow the Sunnah."

The Soul Is Our Foundation

So much of the *dhulm* that is done today by Muslims striving to restrict the mercies of Allah in the lives of believers who choose unpopular marriages—whether in a union that is polygyny, intercultural, or one spouse being significantly older than the other—is done in the name of seeking some "greater good."

Oftentimes, the argument that is used to justify this widespread social harm and religious discrimination is that family is the foundation of the society, so we need to make sure that only "healthy marriages" (i.e. marriages we like and agree with) are supported and built in the community.

When you're on the receiving end of *dhulm* being done in the name of some "greater good," you feel the deep injustice of it. But when you're on the delivery end, you don't even process that what you're doing is wrong at all, let alone harming others unjustly.

I wonder when the Muslims as an ummah will return to trusting Allah more than we trust our own emotions, observations, and convictions; and I wonder when we will return to seeing the preservation of the health of our souls as *always* the greater good.

Yet unfortunately, we simply do not have the ability to comprehend what "the greater good" even means if our hearts are unhealthily fixated on guaranteeing certain worldly results for ourselves or others. And we certainly cannot have the "strong community" we dream of if we are unable to fully accept—in heart, speech and action—that a healthy, strong society and community are built on the soul first and foremost, even before they are built on the family.

Family Isn't the Building Block of Society

Several years ago, I read a Facebook status posted by Dalia Mogahed that really resonated with me. In it she said:

> I grew up hearing that "in Islam the building block of society is the family." I heard and read this so often and from so many different trusted sources that I never thought to question it. It was the Cold War Muslim response to Capitalism's hyper individualism and Communism's hyper communalism that erased the need for all institutions, including the family. But I have recently started to doubt this notion deeply. Moreover, I actually believe it is damaging. This post will make many people uncomfortable.
>
> God told the Angels that He would put on Earth a deputy, singular, not a "family." God tells us that on the

Day of Reckoning we will flee from our family. Singular. God said that no soul bears the burden of another's actions. Singular. We will stand before Him naked and *alone*. The Quran continuously address us as single souls, not "family units." We are told that God will never change the state of a people until they change the state of their souls. Not families. But souls. Singular.

So no. The family is not the building block of society and no the most important value is not the maintenance of an intact family at the cost of an individual's soul. Societies crumble because of the state of our hearts, not our divorce statistics.

So here is my alternative: In Islam the building block of society is the heart. Yes, the heart. As the Prophet said, if this is healthy, the individual is healthy, and by extension the family is healthy and society is healthy and whole. This is why we were created. To purify our hearts. This is the Quranic definition of "success." Not the family unit. But the state of one's heart. In fact, members of our family are said to be possible sources of tribulation in the Quran.

Now, The Beloved of God also said that the best among us is best to her/his family. No contradiction. This is a litmus test for a purified heart. But the fundamental building block is still the heart and not the family.

When we get this wrong, people think their own soul and relationship with God is secondary to the "family." That suffering is noble in the cause of keeping a family together at any cost. That committing injustice to one's self and others in the service of a family is justified. No. Family is a means to fulfilling our purpose on earth: to be His custodians on Earth. It is not the end for which we were created. (August 16, 2016).

Harms of Viewing Family As Foundation

In my experience, the most damaging harm of viewing family as the foundation of society is that we unwittingly view the sacrifice of anything that preserves "family" as inherently good—even if that sacrifice involves the emotional and spiritual health of believers, whether individually or collectively.

There are many other harms, but I believe each of them stems from this one. It is often the ideology of "family comes first" that is at the root of so many manmade behavior codes that well-intended Muslims actively support and introduce into our faith, thereby causing so much harm in the private lives of believers.

These manmade codes not only restrict the mercies of Allah with regards to what is allowed in marriage (or in defining whose marriage is valid), they also restrict the mercies of Allah with regards to a person's right to protect themselves from harm, particularly when it is a spouse, parent, or family member inflicting the harm.

25

Beneficial Advice vs. Manmade Behavior Codes

"**B**ut I have a right to my opinion," we often say in defending the advice that we give others or the new behavior codes we introduce or support. "There's nothing wrong with sharing with someone what we sincerely believe is best for them."

While this is true, it is important to, for the sake of our souls, differentiate between offering specific individuals advice based on their personal circumstance, and introducing new rules in the religion that apply to Muslim men and women in general, especially if it invalidates anything that Allah has validated or restricts anything that Allah has made expansive.

Have Taqwaa When Offering Advice

It is true that Islam forbids introducing new behavior codes to replace those of Allah's, as this is misguidance, *bid'ah*, and *kufr*. However, it is also true that the believers—whether amongst the scholars or worshippers—are certainly free to advise certain *individuals* with regards to what they sincerely believe is the best life path for that individual's particular life or circumstance.

In this, it is best for the advisor (whether scholar or worshipper) to supplement his or her advice with saying

"Allah knows best," as is customary amongst the scholars of the Sunnah when offering advice or issuing fatwas. It is also wise and safest to advise any believer to ultimately consult Allah via *du'aa* and *Istikhaarah* before making a final decision on anything they are seeking advice on.

This level of etiquette is necessary in offering *naseehah* because no matter how knowledgeable, correct, sincere, or wise we generally are (or imagine ourselves to be), the truth is that no one—and I mean absolutely no one—knows the unseen reality regarding what is best for another person's life or soul. In this, not a single child of Adam knows which permissible life choice is good or necessary for which person in this world, as this is part of the *ghayb* that is known only to Allah.

For this reason, the believer who fears Allah and is ever mindful that they must meet Him on the Day of Judgment—even if they are being trusted in the position of scholar, sheikh, imam, or spiritual teacher—will always offer advice with humility and *taqwaa*, while bearing in mind their ever-present human fallibility and susceptibility to error and *ghuroor*.

Be Humble and Know Your Limits

Even when issuing a fatwa on an issue or engaging in permissible *ijtihaad*, a qualified scholar himself is aware of the human limitations and religious restrictions on his Islamic "ruling."

This is because a foundational principle in our merciful *deen* is that no believer—no matter how ignorant he or she is in comparison to the one offering advice—is obligated to follow any human being (no matter how knowledgeable and scholarly) in anything that he or she genuinely believes is incorrect in front of Allah or genuinely harmful to his or her individual life and soul.

Protecting Your Soul

In any case, any advice offered by anyone should never involve the assumption (whether stated or implied) that anything from the Qur'an or prophetic teachings is inherently harmful to a believer's life. This is because we never need to be protected from the guidance of Allah.

However, we do need to be protected—consistently—from the misguidance of human beings. This is the case whether the advisor carries the label scholar or imam, or the advisor is considered a layperson or worshipper.

26

You Could Be Wrong, Dear Soul

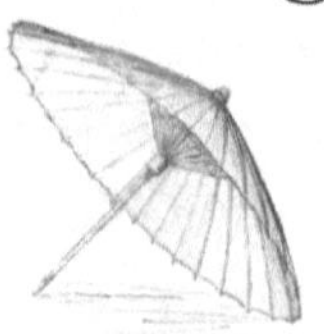

When we are reminded to be conscious of Allah in respecting the personal and spiritual boundaries of others, especially when offering our misguided advice, personal convictions, or unfounded opinions on the lives and choices of others, the *kibr* in our hearts is often triggered. This *kibr* often manifests as indignant self-righteousness that not only incites us to refuse to accept any critique or disagreement, but to also highlight the faults of the person reminding us to fear Allah. In this, we are committing two spiritual crimes:

> (1) transgressing the boundaries of Allah by sharing advice or opinions that contradict the teachings of Allah or His Messenger (peace and blessings be upon him)
> (2) exacerbating this spiritual transgression by harming an innocent believer for no "crime" other than reminding us to be mindful of the Al-Hakam (The Judge), whom we will stand before on the Day of Judgment and answer for every word we uttered in this world, whether with our tongues or social media accounts

Regarding the first spiritual crime, Allah says what has been translated to mean,

"It is not for a believer, man or woman, when Allah and His Messenger have decreed a matter that they should have any option in their decision. And whoever

**disobeys Allah and His Messenger, he has indeed
strayed in a plain error"**
(Al-Ahzaab, 33:36)

Regarding the second spiritual crime, Allah says what has
been translated to mean,

**"And when it is said to him, 'Fear Allah,' he is led by
arrogance to [more] crime. So enough for him is Hell,
and worst indeed is that place to rest!"**
(Al-Baqarah, 2:206).

Although the second *ayah* most specifically refers to
disbelievers arrogantly seeking corruption and destruction
on earth, the spiritual principle being conveyed in this divine
verse applies to all human beings generally, whether Muslim
or non-Muslim.

Seeking Healing, Humility, and Honesty

Undoubtedly, when we react cruelly to a person sincerely
reminding us to fear Allah, this is generally a sign of either
unhealed emotional wounding or of a spiritual sickness in
our hearts. This is the case even if the person offering the
advice happens to be mistaken in their point of view.

The truth is that a believing heart that is emotionally
healthy or sincerely seeking the pleasure of Allah doesn't feel
repulsed, offended, or threatened by another heart seeking
that same pleasure, irrespective of that person's human
faults, misunderstandings, or disagreements with us upon
this path.

Therefore, when we find ourselves lashing out at
someone, especially publicly, for disagreeing with us or
sincerely reminding us to fear Allah, then this is a sign from
our Merciful Creator that we have some emotional healing
or spiritual purification to do.

In this path of self-betterment, it is helpful and humbling to remember that not a single one of us is 100% perfectly healthy, whether emotionally or spiritually. Therefore, realizing that we are guilty of any of this *dhulm* or *ghuroor* should not be processed as a personal attack on our character or faith. Moreover, we should not react to this realization by falling into despair, thinking we are bad people who have no hope of being "good Muslims."

For certainly, whoever amongst us has air in our lungs and a heart beating in our chest, there is always some internal emotional work we must do and some internal spiritual purification we must undergo. This is because the path to optimal health and success, whether emotionally or spiritually, is a lifestyle more than it is a static goal that can be reached and never revisited again.

Reminder to My Struggling Soul

You are not always on the side of right. This is a personal note I wrote to myself as a reminder to my own soul, and I think it's a helpful reminder for each of us to keep in mind. This is especially the case if we are active online or in our communities, wherein we are fighting injustice or inspiring positive change in the social, political, or religious sphere.

When it comes to community betterment, political involvement, or social justice specifically, it is very important to remember that success is not achieved through only one route. I reflect on this point in my journal:

Once upon a time, community work and activism was about encouraging every person to do his or her part in making the society a better place; and everyone had a role to play, whether it was the mother in her home, the father feeding his family, the preacher on the pulpit, or the protester in a peaceful march. No work was devalued, as activists understood that a community is made up of necessary parts of a complex puzzle—and each piece was respected, as both common sense and wisdom would demand.

Today, much "activism" has become a culture of public shaming, following the faults of others, and making public demands on people's private decisions—and linking innocent people to the crimes of oppressors, for no other transgression than not fulfilling a random activist's narrow definition of "supporting the cause."

Other than witnessing the beauty of true activism amidst this troubling trend, the only thing that gives me peace in the face of this travesty of "social justice" is the reminder that there is a Day of Judgment, and the Master of that Day will call each and every one of us to account for the wrongs we inflict upon each other.

27

Allah Doesn't Wrong Anyone

"I feel like Allah isn't giving me what I deserve," the woman said to me in angry frustration. "All He's ever done is been my personal tormenter."
As I listened to the words of my Muslim sister who was obviously battling some deep emotional and spiritual wounds, I honestly had no idea what to say to her.

Before she'd expressed her frustration to me, I'd already given her my own perspective on how to be patient through the trials of life. In this, I shared some things I'd learned during my own healing journey and from the personal struggles I've battled throughout my life. At the root of each thing I shared was how to nourish your emotional health and preserve your soul, even during the most difficult trials of life. However, in response, the woman was deeply triggered and enraged by my advice.

Till today, I'm not sure which part of what I'd said upset her most. In retrospect, I accept the possibility that I was not displaying the compassion and empathy that I'd intended to with my words. This is a human error that I strive to overcome daily, though I know I can never overcome this human fallibility perfectly.

At the same time, I can't help wondering if there was something deeply triggering about me specifically more than the advice itself. This is a struggle I've faced for so much of my adult life. So many Muslims process me as this "religious person" who couldn't possibly understand what "regular people" are going through.

We're All Struggling

I think sometimes we look at a "religious person" offering us beneficial advice and assume they can't relate to our battles with spiritual darkness, our bouts with emotional pain, or our repeated struggles with falling into repeated sin. But in this, we are so often wrong.

Years ago, I remember reading a post by a spiritual teacher that said something to the effect of, "When people are admiring our spiritual goodness and righteousness, they are really admiring how beautifully Allah is covering our sins."

And *subhaanAllah*, how true that is. None of us are exempt from the difficult internal spiritual battles that afflict the children of Adam, no matter how "religious" or scholarly we are (or are perceived to be). And none of us is safe from battling the dangerous waves of spiritual darkness, no matter how deep and dark those destructive waves are.

Even with something as obviously wrong and spiritually destructive as feeling angry with Allah, no one is safe— except those whom Allah has mercy on him such that they do the daily, arduous work of protecting their soul from obvious spiritual harm.

Feeling Angry with Allah

Today, I wonder if I should've said more to help my sister in faith better weather her spiritual storm. However, the truth is, her words scared me.

Because they reminded me of my own spiritual storms.

So often I've had to remind my hurting heart of the divine truth in the Words of my All-Wise, Merciful Creator when He says what has been translated to mean,

"Surely, Allah wrongs not even of the weight of an atom (or a small ant), but if there is any good [done], He doubles it, and gives from Him a great reward"
(An-Nisaa, 4:40).

28

The Darkness Is Not the Problem

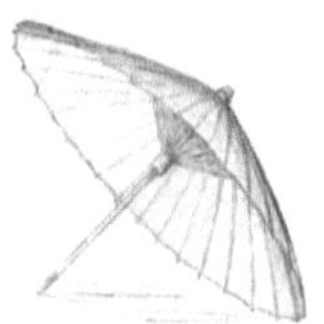

*T*he darkness is not the problem, I wrote in my journal some time ago while reflecting on my own personal trials of the soul. *It will settle upon each of us at various moments in our lives. The problem is only when it reaches you and you reach for it too—instead of reaching for the light…*

"O Allah! Remove this disease from my heart!"

On my healing journey, this is something I'd say often, particularly whenever I felt a tinge of unhealthy pride, ingratitude, frustration, or envy inflaming my heart.

Yes, throughout my life, I've battled each one of these spiritual diseases. I can admit that now. It's something that perhaps years ago, I wouldn't have been able to see as even a possibility—because somewhere along the line I learned that good people don't have "internal darkness."

And I wanted so badly to think I was a good person. But the truth is, I was just a person. A person who *wanted* to be good. Yet I've come to realize this: That's about as close to genuine goodness a human can get.

Success Is in the Struggle

The continuous desire to be good and the subsequent striving toward it each day *is* human goodness.

However, our problem is that on our individual journeys, we focus more on the essence of "being good" than on the essence of being human. Yet both need our focus. But our flawed humanity needs it even more so.

It is in accepting the inevitability of your imperfect humanity that you can more readily embrace the humility that repels pride, that plants seeds of gratitude, that calms frustration, and that extinguishes destructive envy.

A humble heart is not one that fixates on its own goodness. It is one that focuses on its constant, desperate need to connect with the Source of Goodness. That's why when we strive for human goodness, we need to understand that our humanity defines this experience more than our goodness ever could.

But the challenge is that when we take the path toward emotional and spiritual growth, we tend to look down on internal messiness—and we see its signs more readily in the life of others than within our own selves.

My Consistent Prayer

In the Qur'an, Allah says what has been translated to mean, **"So will they not repent to Allah and seek His forgiveness? And Allah is Forgiving and Merciful"** (*Al-Maa'idah*, 5:74). He also says, **"...So ascribe not purity to yourselves. He knows best who fears Allah and keeps his duty to Him"** (*An-Najm*, 53:32).

For this reason, till today, I continue to pray, "O Allah! Remove this disease from my heart!"

Even when I detect no disease in my heart.

Because I know that being unable to detect any sign of spiritual disease is often a sign that it has merely settled more comfortably into the hidden recesses of the heart.

Lesson Seven
Worldly Gardens in the Heart

"It doesn't matter how little or how much you have. In the end, all that will matter is what you did with it—and what you allowed it to do to your heart."
—from the journal of Umm Zakiyyah

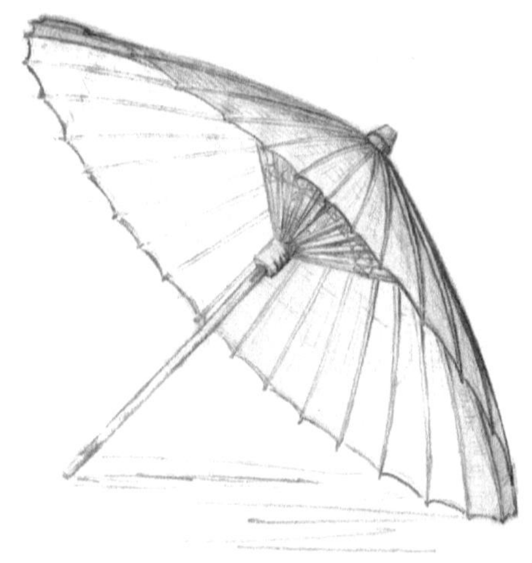

29

What Did You Expect, Dear Soul?

It's a question that I've asked my restless heart on many an occasion over the years: *What did you expect?* Did you expect this worldly life to be full of bliss and ease? Did you expect to get everything your heart desires? Did you expect to face no loss or suffering? Did you expect that wealth, happiness, and success would be yours without being severely tested?

Though I've always understood on an intellectual level that life would be difficult and full of tests, it has been a very difficult journey teaching this same lesson to my heart, hence this reflection in my journal:

> *Knowledge in the mind isn't the same as sincere belief in the heart. It takes only seconds or minutes for the mind to understand something, and a lifetime to instill that same understanding and conviction in the heart. You can teach your mind "knowledge" through reading books and attending classes. But if you desire to teach your heart "knowledge," then the only teaching method that the heart understands is you sincerely and consistently applying that knowledge to your daily life.*

Here are some additional lessons about seeking happiness and success in this world that I've penned in my journal over the years:

Work Ethic, Goodness, and Motivation

Those for whom this world is a Paradise will always see worldly success as a direct reflection of your personal work ethic, inherent goodness, and motivation. Don't make the same mistake.

You might enjoy some comforts in this earthly prison, but in the end, prison is still prison. And there's no inherent goodness in earning "success" in a prison—unless it ultimately earns you absolution and release.

And for the believer, that absolution is God's forgiveness, and that release is *Jannah*.

The Heart Bears Witness

Some people go through severe trials, and it inspires in them humility and servitude. So they call out to their Creator in sincerity, begging for His forgiveness and mercy.

Others go through severe trials, and it incites in them arrogance and entitlement. So they turn away from their Lord in bitterness, angry that He's withholding what they feel they "deserve."

By Allah, the body and spirit suffer, and the heart calls out bearing witness to its own purity…

Or corruption.

It is the heart, not the circumstance, that reflects our truest experiences with life.

So purify your heart, dear soul, purify your heart.

And beseech your Lord's help in this.

Before your heart cries out, bearing witness to a life being lowered beneath the ground…

And begging for an earthly return which will never be granted.

A Ticket to Happily Ever After?

Istikhaarah is not our ticket to "happily ever after" in every circumstance that Allah shows is best for us. This life is only a path to eternal happiness. It is not eternal happiness itself.

So when you pray *Istikhaarah* and then something falls apart down the road, don't look back and wonder if you misunderstood the signs from Allah. You didn't.

But you might be misunderstanding the meaning of Allah decreeing what is best for you. The closest we'll ever get to everlasting happiness in this world is in the relationship we establish with our Creator. And if any trial brings us closer to Allah, it was best for us, even if it's the most painful thing we'll ever experience in this world.

30

Inner Peace Means Abandoning Worldly Pleasures?

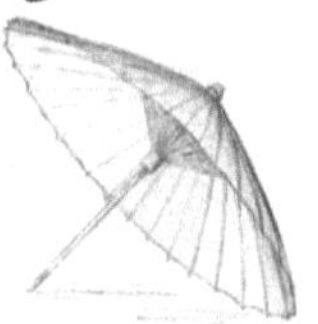

When my *emaan* (faith) was at its lowest, it took me some time to pinpoint exactly what was wrong. And for some time, I sought healing in things that only exacerbated by emotional pain: I read more religious books that condemned the pleasures of this world, I attended more Islamic classes that scorned those who sought personal fulfillment through worldly pursuits, and I abandoned any activities that were not overtly religious. And when my low *emaan* only worsened as a result, I thought to myself, *I must be a bad Muslim.*

It was during Ramadan one year that I, quite accidentally, stumbled upon at least one source of my spiritual wounding and emotional suffering. In keeping with my "religious high," I decided to dedicate my entire Ramadan to only three things: prayer, studying the life of the Prophet (peace be upon him), and reading and reciting Qur'an. But there was only one problem: I had some deadlines for several business and writing projects that I needed to complete, and there was really no other time to do it (especially since I had previously been so neglectful due to my efforts at being a "good Muslim").

So I did what I had to and balanced my time accordingly. And that Ramadan ended up being one of the most spiritually productive and emotionally rejuvenating that I've ever had. That's when I realized what I needed to do to repair my ailing *emaan* for the long-term: I took my life back.

Yes, I continued to enjoy inspirational Islamic books, to listen to heart-touching religious reflections, and to gain spiritual fulfilment through reading and reciting Qur'an. But I was no longer a helpless audience member to my own life, sitting on the edge of my seat struggling to follow the script of those who (I assumed) knew more about my life than I did.

So I resumed my worldly hobbies (guilt free)—reading non-religious books, pursuing creative projects, and exercising and dancing to more than the sound of my own feet.

And almost miraculously, I felt more internal peace. I enjoyed reading the Qur'an more, and I began to love being a spiritually conscious Muslim.

And for the first time in my life, I fully embraced what it meant to have inner peace as a result of not only doing "religious" things, but also enjoying permissible worldly pleasures.

Find Inner Peace in Balance

Yes, it's true. You cannot enjoy inner spiritual peace without having a proper belief in Allah while worshipping Him alone. However, proper belief and worship is the *rooh*—the life and soul—of your worldly life and pursuits, not the opposition to them.

Just as the primary role of the physical *rooh* is to give life to our worldly bodies, proper belief and worship is the spiritual *rooh* that gives "life" and inner peace to our practical lives. Our faith isn't meant to negate or stagnate our worldly life; it's meant to enrich it.

In a well-known hadith from the famous Forty Hadith collection by An-Nawawi (may Allah have mercy on him), Prophet Muhammad (peace and blessings be upon him) said, "…And in the *bud`i* (*halaal* sexual act) of each one of you there is a *sadaqah*." They (the Companions) said, "O Messenger of Allah, when one of us fulfills his carnal desire will he have some reward for that?" He (peace and blessings of Allah be upon him) said, "Do you not see that if he were to act upon it [his desire] in an unlawful manner then he would be deserving of punishment? Likewise, if he were to act upon it in a lawful manner then he will be deserving of a reward" (Muslim).

Why then should we shun the beautiful reward of taking pleasure in *halaal* worldly pleasures while abstaining from *haraam* worldly pleasures? And yes, this path of reward from Allah through enjoying *halaal* worldly pleasures does indeed complement our life of worship. It doesn't contradict it. In this way, it is a path to inner spiritual peace.

To seek inner spiritual peace by abandoning permissible worldly pleasures and doing only what is required regarding spirituality and worship is about as sensible as seeking optimal physical health by neglecting all care for your physical body except what is minimally required to stay alive.

No, it's not sinful to live life this way. However, this level of strict asceticism isn't healthy, physically or spiritually. In fact, it contradicts the Sunnah of our beloved Prophet and Messenger (peace and blessings be upon him). Thus, strict asceticism certainly isn't the formula for optimal spiritual health or enjoying holistic inner peace.

In the Qur'an, Allah says what has been translated to mean,

"But seek, with that [wealth] which Allah has bestowed on you, the home of the Hereafter, and

**do not forget your portion of legal enjoyment
in this world...”**

(*Al-Qasas*, 28:77).

That's why, today, I seek inner peace not only in my belief in Allah and worshipping Him alone, but also in enjoying the permissible worldly pleasures Allah has granted us on earth.

31

Paradise and Prisons

In reflecting on what I learned of the spiritual connection between permissible worldly pleasures and the heart's inner peace, I wrote this in my journal:

If worldly enjoyments have nothing to do with attaining inner spiritual peace, then they have nothing to do with corrupting that inner spiritual peace. Yet we all know the spiritual havoc that sins wreak on our souls, yet we insist on denying the inner peace we gain from worldly pleasures that don't involve transgressions against our souls.

When we insist on denying the blessings of worldly pleasures, we are failing to understand the root of spiritual problems. Spiritual problems aren't rooted in seeking enjoyment in worldly pleasures or in finding a portion of inner peace through them. They are rooted in seeking *only* worldly pleasures or in seeking inner peace at the price of healthy spirituality. In other words, the root of the problem is when we seek to make the prison of this world into the paradise of our hearts.

In a famous prophetic hadith, we are taught this profound spiritual reality in relation to how, as children of Adam, our hearts experience the life of this world: "The world is a prison for the believer and a paradise for the disbeliever" (Sahih Muslim).

So, as believers, when seeking any worldly pleasure, we must understand that we are merely tasting the brief sweetness of a meal enjoyed by a prisoner awaiting release. We enjoy the sweetness of the meal and find pleasure in it, but our hearts are seeking something far more enjoyable, long-lasting, and nourishing for the soul. In this way, we are merely enjoying a brief meal while we await a life outside the constrictive bars of prison, where we can enjoy a more lasting, fulfilling meal in the abode of the Hereafter.

How Much Does Paradise Mean To You?

The reality is that for some of us, attaining Paradise isn't a spiritual priority in our lives. As such, it is only when our hearts become this disconnected from the reality of the Hereafter that seeking to attain inner peace from worldly pleasures becomes potentially harmful.

When something is important to us, we are willing to do the work required to achieve it. We see this clearly in how so many of us eagerly pursue the achievements of this world. Our worldly goal could be becoming physically fit, earning a college degree, becoming a doctor, gaining lots of wealth, or even enjoying the blessing of motherhood or fatherhood.

In these worldly pursuits, we understand that there will be pain and sacrifice, as well as a host of unpleasant obstacles that we must face and work through in order to enjoy this ultimate goal. In fact, we would think someone was deeply ignorant or delusional if they genuinely expected the path to any of these goals to be smooth, painless, and full of only happiness and joy.

Yet when it comes to the path of soul purification for the goal of Paradise, so many of us become discontented or even angry and frustrated if there is any pain, sacrifice, or unpleasantness along the path. When this occurs, the only logical conclusion is that we don't truly believe in what Allah promises regarding the Hereafter. For this reason, the sacrifices necessary to attain it simply are not worth it to us. In contrast, because we believe in the "promises" of success in this world, we work hard toward our goals and are willing to suffer a bit along the way—even as the worldly fruits of our labor are always uncertain, while the spiritual fruits of our labor in the Hereafter are always guaranteed.

Nevertheless, it is important to remember this: True success and happiness—like inner peace and optimal spiritual health—can only be attained through first connecting our hearts to sincere belief in Allah and to a better, more lasting life in the Hereafter.

32

Worldly Gardens of Pride

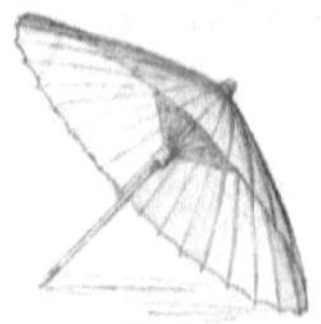

When my daughter was around five years old, I took her to a doctor's appointment with a Muslim doctor I'd found listed in the local business directory. As soon as my daughter and I walked into the examination room, the doctor grimaced and turned her face away from us. "You shouldn't make her wear all of that," the doctor said to us in disgust, referring to my daughter's hijab. "It's oppressive."

"She likes to wear it," I explained. "I don't make her."

"All these women walking around in hijab feel like they're all pious," the doctor continued, wrinkling her nose. "But what good are they doing in the world? You can be a good person without wearing all of that."

Taken aback, I didn't know what to say. I hadn't expected this line of conversation when I'd booked my daughter's appointment.

Contorting her face in distaste, the doctor went on, "I don't pray or wear hijab, but I do a lot more good than all these pious Muslims. Every year, I travel abroad to do medical work for free in poor countries. How many of these women in hijab do that? How many of these Muslims who pray do that? I'm better than they are."

When the doctor noticed my uncomfortable expression, she said sarcastically, "Oh yes, and I'll burn in Hellfire and have my skins roasted over."

Her words sent chills down my spine. I left that doctor's appointment unsettled. The way she had spoken of Hellfire as if it were a joke made my stomach churn. Yet she genuinely imagined she was better than the Muslims who took the reality of the Hereafter very seriously.

Our Worldly Gardens of Pride

Sometimes when I'm doing my Friday reading of *Al-Kahf* ("The Cave," Surah 18 in Qur'an), I think of this doctor, particularly when I'm reading the part about the man who had been given two beautiful gardens. This blessing filled his heart with so much pride that it made him forget his Lord.

Allah says what has been translated to mean (18:32-42):

"And present to them an example of two men: We granted to one of them two gardens of grapevines, and We bordered them with palm trees and placed between them [fields of] crops. Each of the two gardens produced its fruit and did not fall short thereof in anything. And We caused to gush forth within them a river. And he had fruit, so he said to his companion while he was conversing with him, 'I am greater than you in wealth and mightier in [numbers of] men.' And he entered his garden while he was unjust to himself. He said, 'I do not think that this will perish - ever. And I do not think the Hour will occur. And even if I should be brought back to my Lord, I will surely find better than this as a return.'

'His companion said to him while he was conversing with him, 'Have you disbelieved in He who created you from dust and then from a sperm-drop and then proportioned you [as] a man? But as for me, He is Allah, my Lord, and I do not associate with my Lord anyone. And why did you, when you entered your garden, not say, "What Allah willed [has occurred]; there is no power except in Allah"?

Although you see me less than you in wealth and children, it may be that my Lord will give me [something] better than your garden and will send upon it a calamity from the sky, and it will become a smooth, dusty ground. Or its water will become sunken [into the earth], so you would never be able to seek it.'
"And his fruits were encompassed [by ruin], so he began to turn his hands about [in dismay] over what he had spent on it, while it had collapsed upon its trellises, and said, 'Oh, I wish I had not associated with my Lord anyone.'"

We're Better Than They Are?

For the doctor, the worldly "garden" of charitable medical work made her feel superior to all other Muslims, even those who prayed five times each day.

But what is it that makes *us* feel superior to others? As disturbing as the doctor's sentiments are, this sort of *kibr* is not uncommon to the human heart. The truth is that unhealthy pride is something that any human being can fall into. In fact, if we are honest with ourselves, we'll likely find traces of this type of *kibr* in our own hearts. Thus, we have to be in a constant state of self-reflection and daily purification of our souls to guard against this disease taking over our hearts.

Prophet Muhammad (peace and blessings be upon him said), "No one who has an atom's weight of pride (*kibr*) in his heart will enter Paradise." A man said, "O Messenger of Allah, what if a man likes his clothes and his shoes to look good?" He said, "Allah is Beautiful and loves beauty. *Kibr* means rejecting the truth and looking down on people" (Sahih Muslim).

Nearly all of us have something that we take pride in and that can make us feel better than others. Each of us also has the unhealthy human tendency to reject the truth, especially when it comes from someone we dislike, or when accepting that truth means that we have to face some painful truths about ourselves. For this reason, it is crucial that we are in the daily habit of guarding our hearts and souls from this destructive disease.

33

When the "Good Cause" Harms Your Soul

Ironically, pride often takes over our hearts while we're aligning ourselves to a good cause. We can see an obvious example of this in the doctor declaring her superiority over practicing Muslims due to her dedication to the good cause of charitable medical work. However, falling into unhealthy pride is not always this apparent.

Often our unhealthy pride is manifested in the *way* we call others to a good cause, even if we don't openly claim to be better than they are, and even if we don't excuse ourselves from obeying Allah. In these cases, we can see signs of *kibr* in how we treat those who we feel aren't doing enough to support the good cause, or in how far we go in insisting that others take a very specific action in addressing a social or political problem.

When our hearts are afflicted with *kibr*, we become blinded by self-righteous conviction until we begin to dictate the lives of others in the name of solving a social or political problem. We do this even though we have no idea of the *ghayb*, the unseen realities that Allah has decreed in this person's life. Moreover, in our blind conviction, we fail to see that there are multiple ways to address a problem, even in ways we ourselves cannot perceive.

More significantly, in our blind conviction, we fail to realize that Allah has placed on no human soul the obligation to solve every social and political problem that exists on the face of the earth, even those that affect their lives personally. It's simply not humanly possible.

Allah says what has been translated to mean, **"On no soul does Allah place a burden greater than it can bear..."** (*Al-Baqarah*, 2:286). It is unfortunate, however, that we place these burdens on ourselves and others. When we are faced with social and political trials in this world, the most that any of us can do is the best we can based on the knowledge and abilities that Allah has given us.

If Allah gifts us with the worldly blessing of knowledge and ability in addressing a social, religious, or political problem, it is our duty in front of Him to strive our level best to do what we can. Meanwhile, we can humbly share with others how they too can help. However, under no circumstance should we dictate that a person understands the problem like we do, nor should we insist that a person addresses the problem in the exact way that we do. In reminding myself of this, I wrote this note in my journal:

Never ever—and I mean never ever—guilt someone into speaking up or taking action based on your convictions. Even with the clearest and most obvious truth in the world, God tells us, "There is no compulsion in religion" (2:256). If this is God's justice in allowing humans choice in following His way of life, how arrogant it is for us as humans to have less humility in calling to our own.

Once upon a time, activism meant standing up and giving a voice to the silenced and oppressed. But today it too often means standing up and oppressing the silent. No one is ever obligated to speak without knowledge, and only the most ignorant and arrogant amongst us would demand that they must.

Inspiring Change Sans Spiritual Self-Harm

If you know something that others don't, here are two helpful rules of thumb:

1. Share, don't shame.
2. Educate, don't humiliate.

Then trust that God will inspire the hearts of those whom you need by your side in order to triumph over oppression in the end. Victory is not attained through numbers. It is attained through patience, sincerity, and adhering to truth.

Share, Don't Shame

If there's anything I learned in all my travels and being in the company of the religious, the political, and the activist, it is this: Those who respect people most, benefit people most.

Unless our only goal is to show how superior we are to everyone else, then there really is no point in shaming and humiliating people into taking a certain course of action or following a certain point of view. Conveying the actual, real-life benefits of a particular approach or stance is more than sufficient—as opposed to calling people sinful, lazy, or ignorant if they don't do what we think they should.

In the end, it is far more beneficial to share beneficial information instead of shaming and insulting people—if paving the road to a better world is truly our goal.

34

Respecting the People of the Cave

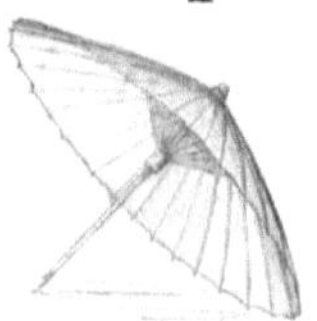

Unfortunately, it is in the realm of addressing political and societal problems that we so often fall into *kibr* and forget our *Rabb* and our own souls as we make specific demands on others. In this, we forget that the Qur'an and the prophetic example offer ample pathways to solving political and social dilemmas, especially when the believers are living in a state of political weakness and religious oppression.

Therefore, it is not our right to demand that any believing soul follow our chosen pathway to political and social improvement, no matter how convinced we are that we are on the side of right.

A Reminder for Our Souls

As a reminder to my own soul and to the souls of my sisters and brothers in faith, I wrote this reflection in my journal:

What right do you have to harass the people of the cave—when Allah praises them in Qur'an? On whose authority do you speak ill of those who retreat from corrupt social and political systems and opt not to participate at all—out of fear for their souls? Are you certain that those you call "lazy" or "ignorant" are not written down as beloved to Allah? Were the youth who retreated to the cave lazy and ignorant— or were they wise and faithful?

No, not every wise and faithful servant of Allah who is praised in His Book rushed to the shelter of a cave to worship Him. But the ones we are instructed to read about every Friday did retreat from a corrupt society over which they had no control.

So, dear soul, consider carefully the Divine reason for this weekly reading before you harass those who only wish to worship their Lord in peace.

Spiritual Lessons from The Cave

In the Qur'anic chapter entitled *Al-Kahf*, which means "The Cave," Allah says what has been translated to mean:

[Mention] when the youths retreated to the cave and said, 'Our Lord, grant us from Yourself mercy and prepare for us from our affair right guidance.' So We cast [a cover of sleep] over their ears within the cave for a number of years. Then We awakened them that We might show which of the two factions was most precise in calculating what [extent] they had remained in time.

It is We who relate to you, [O Muhammad], their story in truth. Indeed, they were youths who believed in their Lord, and We increased them in guidance. And We made firm their hearts when they stood up and said, "Our Lord is the Lord of the heavens and the earth. Never will we invoke besides Him any deity. We would have certainly spoken, then, an excessive transgression. These, our people, have taken besides Him deities. Why do they not bring for [worship of] them a clear authority? And who is more unjust than one who invents about Allah a lie?"

[The youths said to one another], "And when you have withdrawn from them and that which they worship other than Allah, retreat to the cave. Your Lord will spread out for you of His mercy and will prepare for you from your affair facility"
(Al-Kahf, 18:10-16).

I Hope You Vote for Your Soul

Whatever happens during any "election season," I hope you vote for your soul. In this, know that your choice—to vote or not vote for a certain candidate—can only bring about "the greater good" you hope for if the greater good—as defined by our Creator—already exists within your heart and soul.

So if you are using your time blaming innocent people for the crimes of our oppressors because they don't have an "I voted" sticker on their chest, or if you are using your time calling fellow believers hypocrites or wrongdoers because they *do* have an "I voted" sticker on their chest, then understand that you are a manifestation of the very problem you *think* you're solving with your choice.

In the Qur'an, Allah says what has been translated to mean, **"…Indeed, Allah will not change the condition of a people until they change what is in themselves…"** (*Ar-Ra'd*, 13:11). And another translation says,

"…Verily, Allah will not change the good condition of a people as long as they do not change their state of goodness themselves [by committing sins and being ungrateful and disobedient, etc.]…" (13:11).

And both of these meanings are true, as they both point to this unalterable reality, as conveyed in the Qur'an and prophetic teachings: If your heart is corrupt, then everything else you do is corrupt—even if it's a "good deed." And also: Allah is Pure and Good, and He only accepts and blesses that which is pure and good.

So be careful.

And no matter how convinced you are that only *your* point of view is correct, remember this: Our All-Powerful, All-Wise Creator Who is the Master of the Day of Judgment doesn't need your help in bringing about good in this world.

Yes, we *must* do our part, whatever that may be. But don't get it confused. Our part isn't a must because the world needs us. Our part is a must because *we* need us.

In this, we do good to help *ourselves* and to save our own souls from harm in this world and in the Hereafter—not to assign ourselves as the lord and savior of all humanity. This world already has a Lord and Protector, and trust and believe, He doesn't need your voting sticker—or lack thereof—for HIS will to be done.

So, understand, when it comes to issues of permissible disagreement—as politics inevitably are—it is not *what* you do or do not do that determines the good (or bad) outcome for yourself and the world. It is *why* you do it, the spirit in which you do it, and how your heart and tongue react to others who are fearing their Creator differently than you.

Understanding this from the depths of your heart while walking in sincerity and humility is how you vote for your soul. And it is how you do your part in bringing about a better world.

35

Identifying Your Worldly Gardens

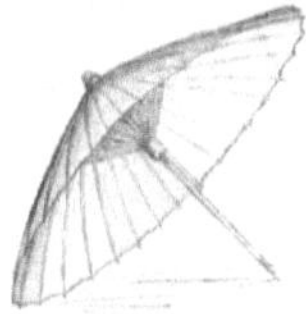

What worldly gardens are you rejoicing in? Your marriage and children? Your wealth and success? Your knowledge and intelligence? Your beauty and status? The "good cause" you are dedicating your life to—and insisting that everyone else joins in, lest you "expose" them for being inferior and uncaring?

Or perhaps there is some other blessing of God you are taking credit for?

Whatever it is that is causing our hearts to forget that we were created from dirt and will return to it—and will be called to account for every blessing we enjoyed in this world—let us reflect on what we have in common with the man in *Al-Kahf* who felt superior to his companion due to what Allah had given him.

And let us also reflect on what we *should* have in common with the youth in the cave—as well as with the Prophet (peace and blessing be upon him) and his Companions.

Why So Eager?

"We're *nothing* like them!" we so often say when we speak of the Prophet, his Companions, and other righteous believers praised in Qur'an and prophetic narrations. But why are we so eager to separate ourselves from them, when Allah Himself points to them as our example? And when Allah commands us in every *Salaah* to pray to be on the Straight Path that they adhered to in their lives?

What then do you think is the purpose of their example, and of this prayer?

Do we really imagine that our brothers and sisters who preceded us couldn't possibly relate to the challenges we face today? Do we really imagine that we can find absolutely nothing in their lives to help us understand our own?

Yet we, like they did before us, face the believers' timeless struggle of holding on to the truth while nearly everything around us—from our *nafs* to the oppressive society in which we live—seeks to pull us away from Allah's Straight Path.

Or do we rush to separate ourselves from their faithful existence because, deep down, we know our dilemmas are no different? Yet the claim of separation allows us to ignore (or deny) our spiritual obligations, claiming we live in "modern times"? When in fact, every era of people lived in modern times, as there is no other possibility for those who are alive during a period in time.

I wonder then what we think we are supposed to learn—other than history—from reading about the youth of the cave, about the plight of those persecuted by Pharaoh, about the *hijrah* from Makkah to Abyssinia and then Madinah? And about every generation calling its people to Allah.

What do you think, dear soul? Are these merely "tales of the ancients"? Or is possible that, within these stories, there are solutions that our Lord wants us to implement today?

If so, then perhaps the "worldly garden" that is inciting *kibr* within us can instead inspire within us *emaan*—sincere, true faith—such that we use this blessing as a means to support ourselves and our brothers and sisters on the path to Allah's Pleasure and the everlasting garden of Paradise.

Also By Umm Zakiyyah

If I Should Speak
A Voice
Footsteps
Realities of Submission
Hearts We Lost
The Friendship Promise
Muslim Girl
His Other Wife
UZ Short Story Collection
The Test Paper (a children's book)
Pain. From the Journal of Umm Zakiyyah
Broken yet Faithful. From the Journal of Umm Zakiyyah
Faith. From the Journal of Umm Zakiyyah
Let's Talk About Sex and Muslim Love
Reverencing the Wombs That Broke You: A Daughter of Rape and Abuse Inspires Healing and Healthy Family
Prejudice Bones in My Body: Essays on Muslim Racism, Bigotry and Spiritual Abuse
And Then I Gave Up: Essays About Faith and Spiritual Crisis in Islam
I Almost Left Islam: How I Reclaimed My Faith
The Abuse of Forgiveness: Manipulation and Harm in the Name of Emotional Healing
even if. bits and pieces from the heart of Umm Zakiyyah
No One Taught Me the Human Side of Islam: The Muslim Hippie's Story of Living with Bipolar Disorder
He Asked About Islam
Alone, But In the Company of Your Lord
Come Back To Allah, Dear Soul: Salaah Coursebook
Dear Soul, It's Time: A Journey of Coming Back To Allah
I'm Divorced Now: Heartbreak and Healing

Order information available at **uzauthor.com/bookstore**
and **uzhearthub.com**

About the Author

Daughter of American converts to Islam, Umm Zakiyyah, also known by her birth name Ruby Moore, is an internationally acclaimed, award-winning author of more than twenty-five books, including novels, short stories, and self-help. Her books are used in high schools and universities in the United States and worldwide, and her work has been translated into multiple languages. Her work has earned praise from writers, professors, and filmmakers. Her novel *His Other Wife* is now a short film.

Umm Zakiyyah has traveled the world training both first-time authors and published writers in story writing. Her clients include journalists, professional athletes, educators, and entertainers.

Dr. Robert D. Crane, advisor to former US President Nixon, said of Umm Zakiyyah, "…no amount of training can bring a person without superb, natural talent to captivate the reader as she does and exert a permanent intellectual and emotional impact."

Professor K. Bryant of Howard University said of *If I Should Speak*, "The novel belongs to…a genre worthy of scholarly study."

Umm Zakiyyah has a BA degree in Elementary Education, an MA in English Language Learning, and Cambridge's CELTA (Certificate in English Language Teaching to Adults). She has more than fifteen years experience teaching writing in the United States and abroad and has worked as a consultant for Macmillan Education.

Umm Zakiyyah studied Arabic, Qur'an, Islamic sciences, *'aqeedah*, and *tafseer* in America, Egypt, and Saudi Arabia for more than fifteen years. She currently teaches *tajweed* (rules of reciting Qur'an) and *tafseer*.

In 2020, she founded an online university to share the life lessons she learned on her emotional and spiritual healing journey. For information on UZ courses, go to **uzhearthub.com** and **uzuniversity.com**

Connect with Umm Zakiyyah online: **uzauthor.com**
Twitter & Instagram: @uzauthor
Facebook: @uzheartsoul
YouTube: uzreflections